Leadership Strategies for Teachers

▶   ▶   ▶   ▶   ▶   ▶   ▶   ▶   ▶

Eunice M. Merideth

SkyLight
Professional
Development

Arlington Heights, Illinois

Leadership Strategies for Teachers

Published by SkyLight Professional Development
2626 S. Clearbrook Drive, Arlington Heights, IL 60005-5310
Phone 800-348-4474, 847-290-6600
Fax 847-290-6609
info@skylightedu.com
http://www.skylightedu.com

Director, Product Development: Donna Nygren
Acquisitions Editor: Sue Schumer
Project Coordinators: Amy Kinsman, Donna Ramirez
Editor: Peggy Kulling
Cover Designer: David Stockman
Book Designer: Bruce Leckie
Proofreader: Heidi Ray
Indexer: Schroeder Indexing
Production Supervisor: Bob Crump

ISBN 1-57517-274-7
LCCCN: 00-131514

2635McN
Item number 1941

Z Y X W V U T S R Q P O N M L K J I H G F E D C B
06 05 04 03 02 01   15 14 13 12 11 10 9 8 7 6 5 4 3 2

Please remember, especially in these times of groupthink
and the right-on chorus, that no person is your friend (or kin)
who demands your silence, or denies your right to grow
and be perceived as fully blossomed as you were intended.

—ALICE WALKER

Excerpt from "A Talk: Convocation 1972" in *In Search of Our Mothers' Gardens: Womanist Prose* © 1983 by Alice Walker, reprinted with permission of Harcourt, Inc.

Contents

Preface

▶   ▶   ▶   ▶   ▶   ▶   ▶   ▶   ▶   ▶

Public education in the United States is an evolutionary phenomenon. For all its problems, in a little more than 350 years, the system has progressed from a meager introduction to scholarship reserved for a few to a system dedicated to developing the potential of all. This evolution has been shaped by orderly social change and crisis, by economic, political, religious forces, and by needs of the individual. It is by no means finished.

Learning, in general, reflects changes in knowledge level and behavior. Like a child who grows, stretches, experiments, fails, and succeeds, an effective educational system must also learn. It must continually add new knowledge as well as respond and adapt to its environment, meeting the needs of current students who have never been more diverse, more intelligent, and more socially challenged. The learning and subsequent reform of an entire educational system, however, cannot be mandated or accomplished by a few talented and powerful individuals. An undertaking this broad must involve a school's entire community in learning, planning, and implementing meaningful change. It follows, then, that leadership among all community members must also be sought, nurtured, valued, and respected. For school systems that have learned the lessons of constructivism and collaboration, teacher-leadership is a natural outcome and a hidden strength. It is the key to the professionalism of teaching and the achievement of all students.

Leadership Strategies for Teachers is designed for and dedicated to all teachers who are committed to their students' learning and their own development. These teachers already help advance school improvement efforts and adopt innovative teaching practices, but teachers rarely see themselves as leaders. Developing that leadership for all teachers who aspire to be their best does not mean empty classrooms or even larger administrations. What it does mean is a community sharing of leadership within a school in order to energize educational endeavors and improve student achievement.

This text offers a REACH model for considering behaviors of teacher-leaders and specific strategies intended to develop comfort with those behaviors. It also explores a variety of roles for teacher-leaders, professional growth and communication skills for teacher-leaders, and networking approaches that connect teacher-leaders. In all cases, research-based theories are followed by concrete strategies with which to translate those theories into practice.

Acknowledgments

▶   ▶   ▶   ▶   ▶   ▶   ▶   ▶   ▶   ▶

It is with deep gratitude that I acknowledge the help and encouragement that made this text possible. I would first like to thank those teachers who, in spite of being stereotyped and often criticized, continue to lead and educate their students. In their classrooms, students not only learn, they also grow.

I would also like to thank three teachers who have been my heroes and ultimately responsible for my career in education. I would like to recognize my mother, Hazel Marie Grice, who taught me the power of resiliency and the satisfaction of creative work. Jane Abel, my high school speech coach, taught me to listen for the music in words and to actually enjoy public speaking. She is a model of just how powerful one teacher who cares about students can be. I also thank Dr. Rosanne Potter, my university professor, who was the epitome of a mentor—she inspired and supported me, and she would accept nothing short of excellence.

I am fortunate enough to have colleagues who have read this manuscript and offered valuable suggestions: Dr. Pamela Richards, Peggy E. Steinbronn, and Hope A. Bossard. I thank them for their patience and insights. I am grateful also for the encouragement offered by family: Pam, Suzanne, Jim, Michael, Sarah, and JorgeAnn. Even Owen, the dog, played his part by lying by the computer for hours.

I am grateful for developmental support from Drake University in obtaining permissions to republish from the educational experts quoted in this work. I would also like to acknowledge Ms. Sue Schumer of SkyLight Professional Development, whose diplomacy and attention to detail made the business arrangements civilized, even pleasant.

Finally, I would like to thank the teachers who have also been students in the Effective Teaching, Learning, and Leadership Program at Drake University. They are the reasons for and behind the text.

—EUNICE M. MERIDETH

Introduction

This book offers an overview of leadership as a dynamic process available to all teachers. Accordingly, it reviews research-based theories applicable to teacher-leadership and presents strategies for the development of leadership skills for all classroom teachers. While designed for teachers, this text can also be helpful for professional developers, administrators, and students of school improvement as they consider the establishment of school-wide learning communities.

Chapter 1 explores teacher-leadership behaviors through the REACH model. Specific strategies in goal-setting, health and wellness, reflective decision making, and conflict resolution as well as a case study involving a teacher's ethical dilemma support these leadership functions (see Figure 0.1).

Chapter 2 describes four roles of teacher-leaders that evolve from being a change agent, to curricular designer, situational leader, and transformational leader. Strategies that bolster these areas of action examine force field analysis, backward curriculum design, and frames of leadership.

Chapter 3 discusses the professional growth and development of teacher-leaders by investigating the concept of professionalism, the five major models of professional development, and collaborative learning and leading. Strategies involving the integration of the inquiry process with thinking skills, card storming, forming and functioning within a collaborative learning group, and mentoring offer practical ways of active involvement with continued learning.

Chapter 4 explains the connections between success in leadership endeavors and communication skills. General concepts of effective communication introduce the specialized topics of communicating with colleagues, communicating with students, and communicating with families. Strategies provide practice in presentation techniques, supportive communication, and a family-school expectations projection.

Chapter 5 discusses connecting teacher-leaders beyond their schools through professional organizations and publications as well as education conferences and exhibits. Strategies outline how to organize a professional development conference or teaching exhibit and provide guidelines for periodical publication.

This text reflects the philosophy that leadership is best developed through the combination of theory and experience that lends confidence to action and satisfaction in defining oneself as teacher and leader.

The REACH Model

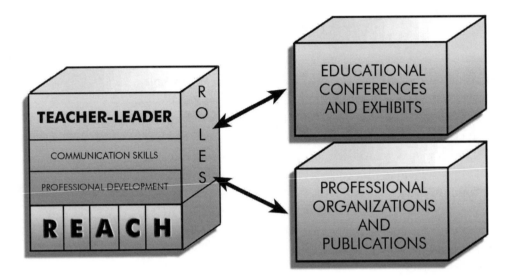

Figure 0.1

SkyLight Professional Development

Teachers as Leaders

▶ ▶ ▶ ▶ ▶ ▶ ▶ ▶ ▶ ▶

In early America when teachers ran their own schools, structured all their own curricula, and recognized their ability to impact the learning of every student who attended school, teacher-leadership was an imperative, not an option. As one-room schoolhouses became multi-room buildings and then multi-building school systems, the status of the teacher moved from expert to employee. The increasing size of schools and their complexities also led to administrative hierarchies and power structures that placed teachers at the lower end of the order. Unfortunately, educational reforms initiatives in the 19th century designed to increase professionalism within teaching only succeeded in increasing school systems' bureaucracy. Popkewitz explains the consequence of these events: "Standardized hiring practices, uniform curriculum policies, and teacher evaluation practices eroded spheres of teacher autonomy and responsibility as there was an increased rationalization of school organization and didactics" (1994, 4). With such a background, it should not be surprising that some teachers do not think of themselves as leaders or may be hesitant to embrace a role they believe may remove them from their classrooms or separate them from their peers.

> The only safe ship in a storm is leadership.
> —FAYE WATTLETON

WHO ARE TEACHER-LEADERS?

Despite extensive research in the general area of leadership, there is not a definitive understanding of contemporary teacher-leadership. Studies that identify leadership characteristics, emphasize strategic planning, and address moral issues and human relations are important sources of leadership theory, but the connection between these theories and the traditional classroom teacher's mission, student learning, is not clear. Moreover, the application of leadership theory in the professional development of teachers has not included all teachers and their classroom practice. In contrast, the REACH leadership model presented in this book approaches leadership inclusively. Because it is designed for professionals, the REACH leadership model is based on theory, but it specifies action. Leadership is not something bestowed upon a teacher to rise above one's role but the fulfillment of that role. Nevertheless, the concept of all teachers as leaders has not been widely adopted by educators at any level.

As early as 1986, the Carnegie Report recommended that school systems identify lead teachers who would exhibit outstanding expertise and teaching skills that could then be emulated by other teachers in the school. The notion of influence over peers and with administrators is echoed by Sirotnik and Kimball as they suggest, "Leadership is the exercise of significant and responsible influence" (1995, 4). Such an interpretation of leadership would recognize a teacher-leader as someone different than most teachers, someone in a special class. Yet Forster asserts that teacher-leadership is both a right and responsibility of teaching professionals. "All teachers must be educational leaders to optimize the teaching and learning experience for themselves and their students; and, as professionals, they are expected to do whatever it takes to make that happen" (1997, 83). Little's definition of teacher-leadership is in accord with the inclusive approach the REACH model advances: "By their presence and their performance, they change how other teachers think about, plan for, and conduct their work with students" (1988, 84). Teacher-leaders place their students' learning as their primary goal and work within their own classrooms to improve student achievement. This is and should be the most important practice of teacher-leadership. Additionally, teacher-leaders focus on their own learning and collaborate with other teachers to accomplish general school improvement.

All teacher-leaders display personal attributes particular to their personalities and teaching styles that mark them as unique; however, this chapter first discusses those behaviors that characterize a teacher-leader and advances the exercise of leadership for any teacher willing to REACH his or her capabilities (see Figure 1.1). Strategies that operationalize the model and apply teacher-leadership behaviors to classroom practice and situations follow.

When taken together all of the elements of the REACH model spell out the type of conduct the ideal teacher-leader exemplifies. The sections that follow discuss each element of this conduct individually for clarity and understanding.

REACH Model for Teacher-Leadership: Behaviors that Together Define Teacher-Leadership

▶ Risk-Taking—Teachers who seek challenges and create new processes

▶ Effectiveness—Teachers who model best practice, professional growth, and heart

▶ Autonomy—Teachers who display initiative, independent thought, and responsibility

▶ Collegiality—Teachers who promote community and interactive communication skills

▶ Honor—Teachers who demonstrate integrity, honesty, and professional ethics

Figure 1.1

RISK-TAKING
E
A
C
H

Early adapters who are willing to try new things, teacher-leaders are risk-takers who relish challenges and pursue professional growth for their own satisfaction and to increase student achievement. These teachers identify with and help solidify the mission statement of a school even as they contribute to the adoption of new approaches to teaching and school improvement processes. Risk-takers have often been called "movers and shakers" because of their responsiveness to problems and their willingness to participate in decision-making, to shake up the system.

Of course, classroom teachers solve problems and make decisions every day, but what makes a teacher become a leader is a take-charge attitude—an internal locus of control—and the confidence and work ethic to set and accomplish goals. Internal locus of control is the perception of control over outcomes, and the belief that one has the competency to perform the behaviors upon which the outcome depends. This is closely related to personal efficacy—individuals' evaluation of their performance capabilities. For example, teachers with strong internal locus of control are confident in their ability to make accurate, proactive decisions. Teacher efficacy, on the other hand, is generally described as a teacher's confidence in his or her ability to positively influence student achievement. The important aspect of both internal locus of control and personal efficacy as each relates to leadership is that they are internal; that is, teacher-leaders believe that outcomes are associated with their actions rather than with luck, fate, or external factors. These internal aspects of control are significant to leadership development because they result in enhanced self-esteem and confidence, each positive motivators of goal and task attainment. Teachers with a strong internal locus of control are also more inclined to suspend gratification, more persistent during difficult tasks, and look to the future with more hope.

Teachers who exemplify leadership typically have a strong work ethic, a firm belief in the dignity of work. "People with a strong work ethic are well motivated because they value hard work; not to work hard clashes with their values" (DuBrin 1995, 44). These are the teachers who are actually energized by teaching, who find themselves tired, but satisfied after delivering a well-planned, activity-oriented day. Valuing hard work is also a characteristic often accompanied by persistence and the ability to find the opportunities in problems—all valuable assets to a teacher-leader.

Students need to see their teachers extending boundaries and stretching their capabilities. Wilson supports the notion that teacher-leaders are risk-takers who challenge processes and seize opportunities, "teacher-leaders go out of their way to find innovative, exciting programs, both for the benefit of their students as well as themselves" (1993, 24). Teachers who are not complacent, but who are excited about learning and expanding their skills through moderate risk-taking provide role models for students venturing into new areas.

R
EFFECTIVENESS
A
C
H

Teacher-leaders are also effective teachers who represent best practice, professional growth, and "heart" (the affective actions of caring, mentoring, and living one's values). Obviously, teacher-leaders must have expertise in their subject areas to establish credibility, but they also need to be able carry out the following activities:

- Establish connections among disciplines
- Know a variety of teaching methodologies to deliver the subject to all students
- Make informed choices about textbooks and materials
- Embrace technology that enhances learning
- Establish relevance to students' lives

Teacher-leaders are also professionals, intellectual and critical learners in the teaching process. Lichtenstein et al. report that the breadth and depth of teachers' disciplinary knowledge empower them as professionals because disciplinary knowledge is the foundation of teacher authority, the stimulus for collegial interaction, and the direction for policy decisions (Lictenstein et al. 1992). Effective teacher-leaders build respect for themselves and their profession as well as a rationale for their involvement in curricular and policy decisions. In fact, Wise and Leibbrand assert that "the expertise of the teacher is the most important school-based factor in determining student achievement" (1996, 202). When classroom teachers model best practice and develop professional expertise, they become effective teacher-leaders because they see leadership as an opportunity to positively affect their own and their students' learning.

In a world where the most powerful resource is information, continuing to grow intellectually is the only way to sustain professional expertise. To this end, effective teacher-leaders practice the following intellectual behaviors:

- They value their own continuing education.
- They assess their teaching in terms of their students' achievement.
- They read and analyze educational research.
- They conduct their own action research.
- They deepen their subject discipline knowledge.
- They update their technology skills.
- They develop curricular materials appropriate to their classes' developmental levels.

These teachers know that their learning did not end as they began their teaching career, but that teaching demands a continued commitment to the interrelationship of subject knowledge and educational practice. Darling-Hammond affirms that "professionalism starts from the proposition that knowledge must inform practice" (1990, 34). Professionalism requires meeting rigorous standards of competence and applying these standards in the classroom. Professionalism also requires supporting and contributing to the good of the whole school.

Leadership, however, is not just a function of the mind; it also demands heart. This aspect of leadership provides self-knowledge and the courage to act upon that knowledge. Sergiovanni explains that, "the heart of leadership has to do with what a person believes, values, dreams about, and is committed to....It is the person's interior world, which becomes the foundation of her or his reality" (1992, 7). They who are influenced by heart not only care for their students, they seek what is best for them and empathize with their concerns. Teacher-leaders also care for others by being approachable and sharing their ideas, time, and support. The willingness of teacher-leaders to sincerely care about others enables them to form strong, positive relationships and to model the values they espouse.

R
E
AUTONOMY
C
H

Autonomous teacher-leaders are not islands unto themselves, but those who display initiative, independent thought, and responsibility. School improvement movements have encouraged teachers to reflect about their own classroom practice. However, teachers have not generally been encouraged to develop and voice individual opinions about curricular and policy matters. In the interest of their "service" profession, too many teachers have been made to feel like servants, taking orders from distant administrators, politicians, and special interest groups who have no knowledge of their classrooms or the needs of their students. For example, Anderson's 1994 report about teachers' views of their influence over school policy presents grim statistics (see Figure 1.2). These statistics are unsettling because they reveal that teachers feel their voices are not heard or valued about issues of curriculum and school policy. Anderson's statistics also communicate teachers' own lack of confidence in their decisions and voices so necessary to leadership. This lack of self-confidence is antithetical to teachers' responsiveness to problems necessary for risk-taking, it reveals doubts about expertise necessary for effective functioning, and it negates autonomy by discouraging independent thought.

Perceived Control over School Policy and Classroom Practice

Percentage of teachers responding they have "considerable influence" in the following areas:

Determining discipline policy	37
Establishing curriculum	35
Determining content of inservice	33
Setting policy on grouping by ability	27

Adapted from *Who's in Charge* by Judith Anderson, 1994, page 3. Used with permission of OERI Research Reports, Washington D.C.

Figure 1.2

Should all teachers simply act as they see fit? Autonomy is not anarchy, and a teacher is still part of a system. Teacher-leaders who show initiative and practice independent thought see school district curriculum outlines and guides and standards as goals. How they choose to design curriculum or meet national or state goals need not be in conflict with the standards movement for school improvement. National and state standards should and do provide goals for student outcomes, but decisions about how to address and access those standards should lie with professional educators within schools. Boyer (1995) maintains that the authority to act on standards rests with local boards. "The board, in turn, after defining the school's mission and key policies, should then place confidence in the principal and teachers to lead, holding them accountable for outcomes" (Boyer 1995, 35). Teacher-leaders who are charged with such leadership are by extension endowed with the autonomy necessary to effectively carry out initiatives that focus on student achievement.

What about teacher accountability?

The flip side of autonomy is responsibility. When teachers assume decision-making roles, they assume responsibility for decisions involving collaborative management and their professional work lives. Consequently, teacher-leaders must accept the responsibility of helping with school improvement plans and addressing students' continuing cognitive and social growth. In addition, they must also accept responsibility for reflection, inquiry, and improvement of their own practice. When teacher-leaders are responsible for themselves, they are truly empowered, finding their power in knowledge. Fay suggests that leadership roles for teachers make this type of empowerment possible and enable teachers to "actualize their professional worth in concrete, fundamental ways" (1992, 58). Teachers who challenge themselves to undertake action research, for example, enjoy a greater confidence by finding the answers they are looking for in classroom questions. Inquiry into educational issues and learning new instructional methods also promote this type of self trust in classroom curriculum decisions, just as sharing results and ideas with others builds community. Responsibility, however, does not mean accepting more work indiscriminately or doing others' work; rather, it means organizing and performing one's own work as a self-manager and leader.

R
E
A
COLLEGIALITY
H

Teacher-leaders who promote community and practice interactive communication skills provide the cement needed to secure the foundation of a school culture. The community of a school is closely related to its culture because the success of the community is dependent upon organizational factors and the quality of its members. Many teachers feel the isolation of their classrooms acutely and wish this could be changed, yet they are reluctant to give up the privacy of that isolation or to violate the privacy of another teacher. Teacher privacy is the uninformed equalizer of a school, the don't-ask-don't-tell unwritten policy within schools. It is a way to believe that all classrooms are the same and all teachers are the same. This is a myth, and teachers know it, but it is a safe myth that absolves teachers of the responsibility of assessing the members of their profession.

To assure quality practice in schools, teachers need to have a community that respects them as contributing professionals. Teachers will, however, have to accept their responsibility within this community to assure quality and give up the sentimental metaphor that calls a school culture a "family." While the notion of family generally carries a warm connotation, it is an inappropriate metaphor for a community of learners because it reinforces a hierarchical system with the head of the family (the principal) in charge of supervising and directing the actions of the other members. In this scenario, teachers are not imagined as the co-parents; they are too often considered the kids. This metaphor also fosters dependence on the principal, negating the autonomy of teachers and putting undo pressure on an administrator to take care of all the problems.

When teachers elect to consider themselves a democratic community of learners and act in a collegial manner, an interdependent atmosphere and attitude replaces a dependent atmosphere and attitude. Members of such communities find that support and sharing do break down barriers and move conversations from problems to possibilities. O'Loughlin's 1992 study also offers an important insight into the value of community learning and leading. Participants of O'Loughlin's study had been inspired to change traditional teaching patterns through individual study, but found themselves frustrated when they returned to their schools because their efforts had no results outside their own classrooms. O'Loughlin concluded that what was needed for real school change was a network of activist teachers who could behave with collective autonomy—a community of teacher-leaders.

To be a teacher-leader within such a community requires problem-solving and conflict-management skills, the ability to establish trust among members, and an orientation toward the good of the entire organization. While an administrator can encourage the organization of a learning community and even participate in it, its success will depend on the school's teachers showing leadership by seeking and maintaining collegial relationships.

As defined by Sergiovanni (1992), collegiality is reciprocal because it involves both support and cooperation—give and take between professionals. "What makes two people colleagues is common membership in a community, commitment to a common cause, shared professional values, and a shared professional heritage. Without this common base, there can be no meaningful collegiality" (Sergiovanni 1992, 91). Collegiality is different from either a social bond among persons who know one another well and enjoy one another's company, or the superficial politeness among persons who are simply tolerating one another. True collegiality involves work goals and an organizational identity that are shared, so that working together for the common good follows naturally. Clearly, collegial leadership necessitates building professional respect for individual effectiveness and strong, interactive communication. Teachers must be able to trust the competencies and intentions of other members of a collegial learning community. When all teachers see themselves as leaders, however, these competencies and intentions are already part of their professional identities, so they are more easily accessed and shared.

R
E
A
C
HONOR

Teacher-leaders demonstrate integrity, honesty, and professional ethics because they understand that teaching and leadership are both linked to intent. Teacher-leaders are not just good teachers, they are good people. Teachers are often uncomfortable when educational conversations turn to values, but the purpose of any academic standard is ethical, centering on the greatest good for students. Moreover, the question so many teachers ask themselves, "Why am I doing this?" has its basis in professional and personal integrity. Boyer points out that as schools combat ignorance they are in the business of teaching values: "Working hard, getting to school on time, completing assignments, and respecting teachers are all values that go to the very heart of education" (1995, 179).

These same values go to the purpose of teacher-leadership. A flashy personality can sometimes masquerade as leadership, but ultimately, people want their leaders to have strong characters and to treat others with respect and dignity. This perspective refutes control management systems in favor of a relationship-oriented approach. A relationship-oriented approach means moving beyond convivial relationships with peers, students, and administrators to personal ones. Waldron et al. write about teaching as a moral activity, noting that power and authority when used simply to control must be replaced by leadership "that must invite, inspire, and accompany young people in their learning, in their process of becoming" (1999, 141).

In an ideal world, all schools would be fully equipped and exciting learning environments. Students would come to school ready and eager to learn. Teachers would facilitate interesting, challenging, and successful learning experiences. Administrators would organize and manage this magical environment so that everyone's needs were met and all community members were happy and fulfilled. In the real world of education, however, the challenge is for all members of a school to work toward the shared goals of school improvement and student achievement. By recognizing and developing their potential as leaders, teachers can ensure their views and voices are taken seriously, and they can become full contributors in a collaborative learning environment.

STRATEGIES FOR **REACH**ING TEACHER-LEADERSHIP

Learning is always accompanied by disequilibrium: the discomfort that is experienced by temporarily inducing an imbalance in the cognitive procedures of perceiving, processing, sorting, and categorizing new information. Equilibrium or balance is restored as the information is acquired and there is a balance struck between what is known and what one needs to know. Oakes and Lipton maintain that "confident learners identify

> Why are you going along with those people? I have to, I'm their leader.
>
> LEDRU-ROLLIN

disequilibrium as something positive—even addictive" (1999, 71). While this proactive view can be admired, it assumes tolerance of uncertainty that is easier to write about than wade through. Accordingly, the strategies that follow are designed to balance the theory information that supports the REACH model with information about how teacher-leaders might apply that theory. These strategies provide activities with which to reflect upon and discuss teacher-leadership behaviors in each of the categories. Case studies offered in this chapter and throughout the book involve fictional characters. Any resemblance of name or situation is coincidental. As teacher-leader information is operationalized, the model in Figure 1.3 begins to take form, illustrating how together the individual elements of the REACH model serve as a base for conduct that defines teacher-leadership.

Teacher-Leadership Model

Figure 1.3

STRATEGIES FOR DEVELOPING RISK-TAKING

As teachers consider new learning, new behaviors, or new roles, they consciously or non-consciously take risks and induce disequilibrium. As this disequilibrium is balanced, there are consequences that can occur at tension points or moments of transition. Caine and Caine predict in such a disequalibrium process, transition points are places that induce uncertainty about the process and the behaviors. At these points, "disequilibrium might lead to reverting to traditional practice, disintegration, or evolution" (1997, 245). To move purposefully toward evolution and avoid disintegration or reversion, a teacher-leader must identify her or his current comfort levels and envision goals that are achievable, believable, and credible—the ABCs of goal setting.

A goal is *achievable* if it is possible in terms of task difficulty, skill, and resources. Achievability can be assessed by asking the following questions:

- How difficult is the goal you wish to reach?
- Does it need to be broken down into smaller tasks?
- What skills do you have in this area?
- What skills do you need to develop in this area?
- What type of resources will it require?
- How will you obtain those resources?

When these questions have been asked and answered affirmatively, one can assume that the goal is possible—it could be achieved.

A goal is *believable* if it feasible in terms of knowledge, time, and values. Reflecting about the feasibility of a goal using the questions that follow clarifies if one is able to address the goal with enough skill to be successful. It also helps establish whether one will be willing to reorder personal and professional concerns to work on the goal.

- Do you have knowledge of what you wish to achieve? Remember, knowledge informs practice.
- Do you have enough time to plan, implement, and assess the goal?
- Does the goal fit within school, community, personal values?

If these questions are answered negatively, teachers need to educate themselves or others about the benefits of the goal before proceeding. If these questions are answered positively, the success of the venture may not be assured, but it is at least feasible.

A goal is *credible* if it desirable, important, worthy of pursuit.

- Will the goal enhance your teaching and the learning of your students?
- Will the goal enrich your life and/or the lives of your students?
- Will the goal contribute to the mission of the school?
- Is the goal necessary to continue to grow academically, socially, emotionally, or morally?
- If it is an educational goal, is it grounded in research?
- How applicable are the research results to your classroom?

Teachers may face encouraged or imposed goals that they know are inappropriate for the developmental needs of their students or goals. They may be asked to strive toward some goal in a misdirection of energy because attaining them has not been proven to increase student achievement. However, when the answers to the questions above indicate that the goal is credible, it is time to take a risk and pursue that goal vigorously.

The strategy that follows gives potential teacher-leaders some practice employing the key questions central to the ABC's of Goal Setting as they frame their teaching-related goals (see Figure 1.4). With one's aim focused and the elements of the goal clear, decisions are informed and risk-taking is more manageable.

The ABCs of Goal Setting

What is the goal or outcome that you seek? With that goal in mind, answer the following questions.
Your Goal:

The Goal Is Achievable

▶ How difficult is the goal you wish to reach?

▶ Does the goal need to be broken down into smaller tasks?

▶ What skills do you have to meet the goal and accomplish the tasks?

▶ What skills do you need to develop to meet the goal and accomplish the tasks?

▶ What type of resources will the goal and/or the skills needed to meet it require?

The Goal Is Believable

▶ Do you have knowledge of the goal you wish to achieve?

▶ Do you have enough time to plan, implement, and assess the goal?

▶ Does the goal fit within school, community, and personal values structure?

The Goal Is Credible

▶ Will the goal enhance your students' learning and your teaching?

▶ Will the attainment of the goal enrich your life and/or the lives of your students?

▶ Will the goal contribute to the school's mission?

▶ Is the goal necessary to continue to grow academically, socially, emotionally, or morally?

Figure 1.4

Critical Goal Review ▷ ▶ ▶

Jensen asserts that "teaching is a high-risk career. If you're not risking, you're not growing; and if you're not growing, neither are your students" (1995, 170). With this quote in mind, one can use the Critical Goal Review Chart to (1) identify goals; (2) analyze the goals using the ABC's of goal setting on a scale from one to five; and (3) predict the amount of risk that achieving the goals would involve on a scale from one to five. While there are not scores that assure successful goal setting, the ranking applied within each category can help balance the elements of setting goals with the risk they demand.

Critical Goal Review Chart

Your Goals	Achievable	Believable	Credible	Level of Risk
Student Learning:				
Personal Learning and Growth:				
Curriculum Development:				
Learning Community:				

Figure 1.5

STRATEGIES FOR DEVELOPING EFFECTIVENESS

As effective teacher-leaders develop their expertise, engage in professional activities, and demonstrate heart, they are advancing a teaching-for-understanding paradigm. Within this paradigm, a teacher recognizes the need for a strong understanding of her or his subject matter and well-developed pedagogical skill to present that subject well. The major focus of teaching-for-understanding is student learning that is addressed by teachers whose role evolves from the "sage on the stage" to "guide on the side." If teachers are to change their roles in the classroom to be more effective, they must also help students change their traditional roles from passive learners to active scholars who seek understanding of concepts and assume more responsibility for their own learning. Strategies that promote effective teaching-for-understanding follow:

1. **Scaffolding for students.** Scaffolding tasks for students allow them to be successful at their current level and to reach beyond that level to tasks that would initially be beyond their abilities. Scaffolding strategies, like construction scaffolding, provide support at the current level to reduce failure, but challenge students to reach out by encouraging them to try new things. A teacher using scaffolding begins by supporting and sharing the task, then gradually transfers control of the learning task to the student.

2. **Learning tasks that reflect authentic activities.** Authentic activities in the classroom mirror "work-world" applications and help attach a sense of reality to a concept or problem. The authentic nature of a task often influences the motivation to learn and facilitates students' sensitivity to their own higher-order thinking by adequately answering the popular question, "Why do we have to do/learn this?"

3. **Discussions that represent knowledge as constructed.** Teaching-for-understanding invites both teacher and students to contribute to learning efforts by constructing knowledge together. This approach teaches students research and questioning skills by asking them to supply evidence and support for their ideas. It also helps them integrate new knowledge with what they already know as well as come to shared understandings with their teacher and classmates.

4. **Progressive transference of the responsibility for learning to the learner.** Helping students assume more responsibility for learning increases their belief in their ability to succeed and make confident judgments. Mastery experiences as part of this strategy should not be too easy or students will come to expect instant and constant success. In addition, progressive transference requires reflective discussions that probe student thinking, and problem-solving skills that look for creative alternatives.

Implementing teaching-for-understanding strategies requires potential changes in teachers' content and methods knowledge, pedagogical skills, and assessment of the effectiveness of their teaching and their students' learning. The Effective Teaching-for-Understanding Map on the following page provides an instrument with which teachers can map comparisons between present classroom practice and plans for change across the strategies outlined above.

Effective Teaching-for-Understanding Map ▶ ▶ ▶

Teacher-leaders can complete an Effective Teaching-for-Understanding Map by examining the strategies listed at the left of the chart and mapping their potential classroom application. Completing the present and future prompts under these strategies' intersecting components (knowledge, skills, and assessment) connects current ideas and levels of practice with future direction. One very important result is the comparison of aspirations (the future) with actions (the present); this comparison allows teacher-leaders to judge where professional development might best increase their effectiveness.

Teaching-for-Understanding Map

Strategies of Effective Teaching-for-Understanding	Knowledge		Skill		Assessment	
	Action	Aspiration	Action	Aspiration	Action	Aspiration
	I know...	I would like to know...	Skills I have...	Skills I would like to have...	What I do...	What I want to do...
1. Scaffolding that encourages student success						
2. Learning tasks that reflect authentic activities						
3. Discussions that represent knowledge as constructed						
4. Progressive transference of the responsibility for learning to the learner						

Figure 1.6

Health and Wellness for Effective Teacher-Leaders

Good health evolves from constructive health choices that improve the quality of life, best measured by an individual's sense of well-being and physical fitness levels. These health choices contribute to the effectiveness of teacher-leaders and model their commitment to mind-body education. In addition, wellness and physical fitness programs help teachers recognize and deal with major stressors in their personal and professional lives.

Stress is the nonspecific adaptation of the body to stimuli. There are two types of stress: stress that is perceived as a result of a negative phenomena is called *distress*; stress that is perceived as a result of a positive phenomena is called *eustress*. There is a curvilinear relationship between stress and performance (see Figure 1.7). Therefore, it is important to remember that any change that a person experiences generates stress; change from a positive event still introduces stress.

Effects of Stress on Performance

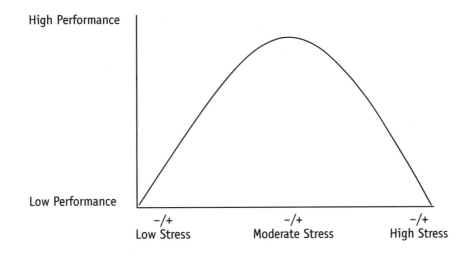

Figure 1.7

Teachers need to be sensitive to the amount of change in their daily schedules and regimens, because too little stress can result in boredom and apathy, while too much stress can cause burnout or breakdown. It is just as stressful for the body to win $100,000 as to lose $100,000.

The two best ways to deal with either type of stress are either deal with how one perceives events that cause stress (a person may envision herself or himself on a calm beach instead of in a hurricane), or detect and release physiological symptoms that are caused by stress (headaches, high blood pressure, indigestion, etc.). Truch (1980) advocates a stress management program that integrates relaxation techniques, routine exercises, a healthy diet, and a positive attitude to increase performance efficiency. The benefits of getting regular exercise, maintaining a positive attitude, and following a sensible diet are well documented. Teachers can try the relaxation exercise that follows to increase their effectiveness and to take a well-deserved break.

DEEP RELAXATION EXERCISES

Muscles have only two functions; muscles contract and relax. Stress induces contractions within muscles, which induces bodily tension. Conscious relaxation is a skill that can be learned through practice. Relaxation techniques control the amount of tension in the muscles by employing the three Rs of relaxation:

1. Reduction of mental activity
2. Recognition of tension
3. Reduction in respiration.

Some examples of the conscious relaxation exercises are shown in Figure 1.8.

Progressive Relaxation   Before one can consciously relax a muscle, one must first tense it. As part of this technique, contract all the muscles in the body and then progressively relax the muscles, large muscles first, and then later the small ones. Contractions are gradually reduced in intensity until no movement is visible.

The purpose of this method is not only to reduce tension that is present, but to note the feeling of tension, so that one can choose to "let go" of the tension and relax the muscles.

Sample Relaxation Routine

1. Contract hand and make a fist; relax the hand.
2. Bend elbows and contract the biceps muscle; relax arm.
3. Raise eyebrows and wrinkle forehead; relax eyes.
4. Make a face; wrinkle you nose and squint; relax the face.
5. Clench teeth; relax jaw.
6. With teeth apart, press lips together and press tongue to the roof of the mouth; relax.
7. Contract shoulders to ears; relax shoulders.
8. Contract abdomen; relax abdomen.
9. Pull instep and toes toward shin; relax legs.

Figure 1.8

Imagery Technique   This technique involves thinking autogenic phrases that help one visualize feelings. Autogenic refers to a state of attention that centers on a sense of heaviness or warmth for a particular part of the body. For example, imagine you are a limp, rag doll with no one to hold you up or hold you in. Another common reflection is to imagine yourself "floating" in air or in water. Whatever the autogenic visual used, imagery is actually a form of self-hypnosis that removes the tension by taking the mind off anxieties and consciously placing it elsewhere, thereby relaxing the muscles. Imagery techniques celebrate "mind over matter," allowing easier breathing and relaxation.

STRATEGIES FOR DEVELOPING AUTONOMY

Moving from educational employees to teacher-leaders requires knowledge and awareness of what is currently happening in the classroom as well as decisions about what should be happening. Danielson (1996) estimates that teachers make up to 3,000 nontrivial decisions during one school day. This can be exhausting, or it can be informative if approached in a reflective manner. Reflection is a vital part of teacher-leaders' decision making, although some decisions may be made before instruction, during instruction, or after instruction. Costa (1991) explains these decisions or thought-processing actions as phases: the planning or *preactive* phase, the teaching or *interactive* phase, the analyzing and evaluating or *reflective* phase, and the application or *projective* phase (see Figure 1.9).

These phases of decision making are important to developing autonomy and practicing responsibility because they trace the instructional process from planning through implementation to improved planning and instruction. Reflective decision-making enables teachers to assess past decisions to make better decisions in the future. Reflective decision making is an essential activity that separates a teacher from a teacher-leader.

Reflective Decision Making

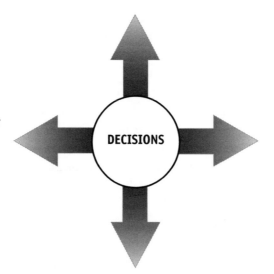

PREACTIVE PHASE: All of the decisions that you will make to plan instruction—standards, benchmarks, student individual needs, resources, procedures, assessment, motivation, etc

PROJECTIVE PHASE: All of the decisions that will project your reflection and analysis into further planning and instruction that follows.

DECISIONS

INTERACTIVE PHASE: All of the decisions made while actually instructing—student comprehension, student attention, individual questions, lesson focus, change of direction, etc.

REFLECTIVE PHASE: All the decisions made after you reflect about, analyze, and judge the decisions made in the first two phases.

Reprinted from *Creative Conflict,* a paper presented at Drake University, October 1991 by D. Johnson and R. Johnson. © 1991 by Johnson and Johnson. Reprinted with permission.

Figure 1.9

Reflective Decision Making for Teachers

The purpose of this strategy is to learn more about the decision-making process and how teachers approach it. Use the following questions to elicit a discussion with another teacher about the decisions he or she can remember during one particular day. Compare the responses of your teacher-interviewee to the responses you would make. Did all four phases occur? These types of reflections would be valuable as part of a teaching portfolio or journal to record one's journey and growth. The following offers sample question teacher-leaders may use to refine their personal decision-making processes.

Preactive Phase: What decisions do you make before instruction?

- What is knowledge?
- How should knowledge be taught/learned?
- What resources/materials do you need to use?
- How do you establish benchmarks? Assess instruction?
- Type of lesson? How do you choose activities?
- What effect do my classroom management policies have on instruction?

Interactive Phase: What decisions do you make during instruction?

- How do you interact with your students?
- What routine decisions do you make?
- How are your classroom decisions based on school policy?
- Are teachers responsible for student learning?
- How do you engage your students in their own learning?
- If all teachers were leaders, how would their classrooms change?
- How are teaching and learning related?

Reflective Phase: How do you reflect and analyze decisions and instruction?

- What learning occurred in my classroom?
- Will I review any of the teaching/learning tomorrow?
- How can I deal with _____'s behavior today?
- What is _____ real problem?
- Will I make any revisions in my plans for tomorrow?
- What resources would I change in my delivery?
- What have I learned about my teaching today?

Projective Phase: How will decisions made during reflective phase impact future teaching?

- What do I do well when teaching?
- What will I change about my teaching?
- What do I think about my students?
- How can I impact students' learning?
- How current am I with my subject/area?
- How can I function as a teacher-leader?
- How can I share what I know with parents, administrators?

Reflective Decision Log ▶ ▶ ▶

Periodically keeping a decision log as part of a teaching portfolio helps create an awareness of the kinds of decisions made daily. Teachers can record their most important reflective decisions for one week and reflect upon the decisions to find any patterns that might occur.

Reflective Decision Log

Days	Preactive Phase	Interactive Phase	Reflective Phase	Projective Phase
Monday				
Tuesday				
Wednesday				
Thursday				
Friday				

STRATEGIES FOR DEVELOPING COLLEGIALITY

The ideals of collegiality (support and cooperation among colleagues) can be threatened when the reality of conflict among colleagues emerges. Conflict occurs when an idea or behavior blocks or prevents the effectiveness of another idea or behavior. Conflicts are inevitable because individuals, their ideas, and their interests are different. The absence of conflict, however, is apathy and indifference—a negative state that does not encourage change and development. Because conflict arises from differences, it can be difficult and seem very personal. On the other hand, it can be constructive when both parties accept a win-win situation. For example, when a conflict has been discussed and settled to the satisfaction of all the parties involved, the ability to work cooperatively and manage future conflict is improved.

How does this happen? Clearly, establishing an atmosphere of trust creates the base for constructive conflict, but Johnson and Johnson (1991) aid the process with their rules outlining how to be constructive while being critical (see Figure 1.10).

If teacher-leaders are to move beyond the status quo, they will need to be critical. Being critical, however, does not need to be destructive. The Rules for Constructive Criticism below establish a way to disagree about ideas without attacking persons who have those ideas. They also stress understanding through information and analysis of data and experience so that collegial relationships can actually foster risk-taking, improve higher-order thinking, and nurture autonomy—all part of the REACH paradigm.

Johnson and Johnson's Rules for Constructive Criticism

1. I am critical of ideas, not people. I challenge and refute the ideas of the opposition, but I do not indicate that I personally reject them.
2. Remember, we are all in this together. I focus on coming to the best decision possible, not on winning.
3. I encourage everyone to participate and to master all the relevant information.
4. I listen to everyone's ideas, even if I don't agree.
5. I restate what someone has said if it is not clear.
6. I first bring out all ideas and facts supporting both sides, and then I try to put them together in a way that makes sense.
7. I try to understand both sides of the issue.
8. I change my mind when the evidence clearly indicates that I should do so.

Reprinted from *Creative Conflict* a paper presented at Drake University, October 1991 by D. Johnson and R. Johnson. © 1991 by Johnson and Johnson. Reprinted with permission.

Figure 1.10

Making Conflict Constructive ▶ ▶ ▶

Teachers can consider the case study that follows and discuss their reactions with a fellow teacher and an administrator.

■ CASE IN POINT ■

Conflict Over Change

Steve Greeley is a fifth-year teacher at Edmonds Senior High School and has been elected to the new faculty-administration management committee to implement site-based management. He has always been considered a teacher-leader by administrators and his fellow teachers with a pleasant personality and has attended a management training conference. After this training, Steve was eager to begin work. But at the very first meeting of the group, differences about the scope and timing of the change divided the group. Discussion deteriorated into personal accusations and put-downs. Even Steve did not escape this criticism. Some members felt he had been favored because he had been sent to the conference.

Steve tried to help by telling the other members what they needed to do to make site-based management successful. It seems they were not impressed, even though he knew the directions were right (he wrote them down at the training session). The meeting was adjourned with little action but lots of hostility. Steve is talking over this problem with you, his friend and colleague.

- What advice can you give him about handling conflict?

- Which Rules for Constructive Criticism did the group use?

- Which Rules for Constructive Criticism did the group break?

- Does Steve exemplify the REACH model of teacher-leadership?

- What would you do in this situation?

Take time to process the case study by using the leadership strategies and theories that have been presented thus far. What did you discover? Perhaps you recognized that in taking the assignment, Steve was willing to be a risk-taker and interested in adopting a teacher-leadership role within the school. However, in his enthusiasm for the task, he forgot to extend professional courtesy and roles to his colleagues. He did not see them as effective and autonomous with ideas of their own, but began giving them orders about what needed to be done. He has also ignored the Rules for Constructive Criticism by not encouraging an active exchange of opinions and information. At this point, he might use e-mail to mend fences, gather information, and share the Rules for Constructive Criticism so that the next meeting might be more productive.

STRATEGIES FOR DEVELOPING HONOR

Discussions about the ethics of teaching professionals are not meant to place one person's set of personal values above another's. The ethics of teaching are currently based in what is termed a *public ethic*: those values and beliefs (including fairness, integrity, justice, and liberty) appropriate in a liberal democracy. However, Strike extends the notion of an individual with a public ethic to the ethic of a community in two ways: (1) A community is not only committed to certain values as ends (respect, for example), but the value of respect is a part of the ethical make-up of the community; and (2) "It is the business of schools to create citizens for a liberal democratic society and to produce and reproduce this society" (1996, 874-875).

In the interest of pursuing an ethical ideal for the community of teachers, the 1975 Representative Assembly of the National Education Association passed a *Code of Ethics of the Education Profession*. The preamble to this code can be found in Figure 1.11.

Teacher-leaders should value ideals, striving always to demonstrate integrity, honesty, and professional ethics. The Preamble reminds teacher-leaders that they act honorably for themselves, their colleagues, students, parents, and members of a wider community.

National Education Association Code of Ethics

Preamble

The educator, believing in the worth and dignity of each human being, recognizes the supreme importance of the pursuit of truth, devotion to excellence, and the nurture of democratic principles. Essential to these goals is the protection of freedom to learn and to teach and the guarantee of equal educational opportunity for all. The educator accepts the responsibility to adhere to the highest ethical standards.

The educator recognizes the magnitude of the responsibility inherent in the teaching process. The desire for the respect and confidence of one's colleagues, of students, of parents, and of the members of the community provides the incentive to attain and maintain the highest possible degree of ethical conduct. *The Code of Ethics of the Education Profession* indicates the aspiration of all educators and provides standards by which to judge conduct.

Figure 1.11

An Ethical Dilemma ▷ ▶ ▶

Imagine yourself as an invisible observer of the following situation which describes one teacher's ethical dilemma.

■ CASE IN POINT ■

Equity versus Equality

Mrs. Ann Davis watched the last of her students leave the middle school language arts classroom. She knew she was a dedicated, constructivist teacher who centered her instruction around the needs of her students, but the students and their abilities were so diverse! Just yesterday she dealt with a classroom conflict between a traditional student, Craig Kelly, and a special needs student, Robbie Thompson. Craig felt that the assessment of his unit project was more rigorous than Robbie's and declared the grading UNFAIR. He also accused Mrs. Davis of cheating him and favoring Robbie.

Today, Ann Davis would be dealing with Craig's mother who had requested a conference and an explanation. As Mrs. Thompson arrived, Ann took a deep breath and reminded herself of all of Craig's positive characteristics and her own ethical responsibilities to both students as a classroom teacher-leader.

Process this case study by role playing the conference between Ann Davis and Mrs. Thompson with another teacher. Then discuss the following questions that analyze how this teacher should practice honorable conduct.

- What in your opinion are the ethical decisions that complicate grading?
- Should special needs students in a traditional classroom enjoy special consideration?
- Does equal treatment assure equity of opportunity or outcome?

Looking Back/REACHing Forward ▶ ▶ ▶

Chapter 1 introduced the REACH model as a means of considering behavior that characterizes teacher-leadership. Many teachers practice some of these leadership behaviors either consciously or nonconsciously. Teachers-leaders can use the following as a tool to reflect upon their own practice during the past sixty days.

In what ways have you evidenced the following behaviors related to teacher-leadership?

Risk-Taking:

Effectiveness:

Autonomy:

Collegiality:

Honor:

List some of the ways you can improve or enhance your leadership behaviors.

Risk-taking:

Effectiveness:

Autonomy:

Collegiality:

Honor:

Teachers-Leaders in Action

▶   ▶   ▶   ▶   ▶   ▶   ▶   ▶   ▶   ▶

Because leadership is defined by the interplay of a person, a learning community, and/or a situation, it has cultural meaning that is unique to time and place. Leadership is not a constant concept, but evolves to meet goals and fulfill roles that are as complex as teachers' dealings in their classrooms and within their schools. The interactions of people and situations provides different roles and experiences for teacher-leaders—as change agents, as curriculum leaders, as situational leaders, or as transformational leaders. The availability of these experiences and the acceptance of these experiences may vary from teacher to teacher and time to time, but all teacher-leaders practice REACH behaviors through roles. It is the combination of learning about leadership and successful experiences in different leadership roles that lends confidence and vision to action and adds another element to teacher-leadership (see Figure 2.1).

TEACHERS AS CHANGE AGENTS

Change is a process, a predicament, an exciting dance in which participants weave and interact, balancing the movement of the participants as a whole through individual skill and flexibility. However, even exciting and promising educational change is only theory until it has been implemented and sustained. It is in the practice that change becomes a positive force or a discarded fad. Planning for effective educational change involves decisions in three basic areas: curriculum (the content of the innovation), instruction and resources (the context of the innovation), and governance (the control of the innovation). Although these three areas are basic, the

> Progress occurs when courageous skillful leaders seize the opportunity to change things for the better.
> —HARRY S. TRUMAN

The REACH Model

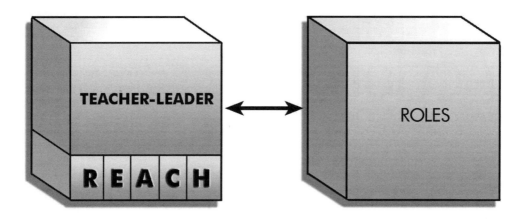

Figure 2.1

decisions that affect them are not simple; instead, they are complicated and require careful and sophisticated decision making. Choices and direction in curriculum and instruction, resources, and governance affect all the systems within a school and can generate systemic change.

Historically, schools have approached change as a series of independent innovations implemented over time. Systemic change, on the other hand, is a relatively new paradigm in educational planning and thinking that analyzes the big picture by observing patterns and relationships of interacting systems. For example, a systemic change perspective views a pattern of behavior problems in a classroom as a stimulus to activate an examination of the classroom and classroom management as a whole. Traditional discreet innovation views the same situation in terms of just an individual student acting out. Systemic thinking that supports change is also a paradigm shift for teachers who may be unused to thinking of the teaching and learning in their classrooms as functions of the school as a whole. But this type of holistic thinking is necessary for collaborative relationships and control that make educational change a shared process. Most teachers would agree that any significant school change is shared (intentionally or unintentionally); however, the collaborative control indicative of systemic thinking and change offers teachers decision-making opportunities previously regarded as within the realm of administrators, directors, and consultants. This shared control requires shared leadership wherein teacher-leaders not only have the possibility, but they also have the responsibility to become agents involved in shaping change.

In their professional lives, teachers experience an astonishing amount of change—new students, new knowledge, new technologies, new classroom arrangements, new social responsibilities, new administrators, new organizational structures. Because of all the emphasis on and excitement about "newness" in change, it is easy to lose sight of the fact that change is a transitional process that also involves loss. When accomplished dancers modify their dance routines, certain steps are changed or even abandoned; the grace and agility with which the group moves together may be temporarily affected, and anxiety and uncertainty may rise. So too participants in change experience excitement, energy drain, and apprehension. Consequently, change may be dangerous, exhilarating, and involve some grieving all at the same time. Tertell et al. maintain that facing real change is a heroic task: "It requires individuals to give up their old ways and to make the terrifying leap into a new way of being or doing" (1998, xxi). The change process, however, also rewards the brave and adventurous with new experiences and the possibilities of innovative alliances and practice. In this way, the change process actually reinforces risk-taking and autonomy even as it provides different collegial opportunities for professional interaction.

The change process, then, can be viewed by teachers either from a positive or negative perspective. In a positive light, change is seen as necessary to continue to evolve and is embraced proactively. From a negative viewpoint, change is seen as a threat to social and cultural patterns of stability and meaning and is approached in a reactive manner. One thing is certain—not everyone will be comfortable with change. Moreover, opinions about the need and value of change will themselves change. Hall and Hord (1987) describe the difficult process encountered by professionals undergoing educational change as Stages of Concern that move from uninterested and uninvolved in the change to highly involved and supportive of the change.

- Stage 0—Awareness: Little concern about or involvement with the innovation
- Stage 1—Informational: A general interest in and awareness of the innovation
- Stage 2—Personal: Individual is uncertain about the demands of the innovation
- Stage 3—Management: Attention is focused on the processes and tasks of using the innovation
- Stage 4—Consequence: Attention focuses on impact of the innovation on one's own students
- Stage 5—Collaboration: The focus is on coordinating and cooperating with others to use the innovation
- Stage 6—Refocusing: The focus is on exploration of more universal benefits from the innovation

(Hall & Hord 1987, 60)

Relating Teacher-Leadership to Hall and Hord's Stages of Concern

Stages of Concern	Individual Facing Change	Leading Change
Stage 0: Awareness	• Little concern about or involvement with information that is not personally relevant • Aware of information about change	• Create sensitivity to the information and establish relevancy by sharing information about how the change can positively affect student learning
Stage 1: Informational	• Aware of the innovation • Has a general interest in learning more details • Has little concern for his or her potential role in implementing the innovation	• Provide information and details about the innovation • Arrange for teachers who are currently involved with a similar innovation to share their perspectives
Stage 2: Personal	• Aware of the possibility of change • Centers her or his concerns upon the personal effects of implementation	• Furnish professional development that emphasizes implementation • Outline how the reward structure of the organization will respond to implementation of the innovation • Foster reflective thinking about change
Stage 3: Management	• Attention turns to processes and tasks of using the innovation • Management issues related to organizing, scheduling, and time become the greatest concerns	• Acknowledge that any change in a comfortable routine is difficult • Provide support for new routines • Arrange release time for mentoring and consultation
Stage 4: Consequence	• Attention focuses on the impact of the innovation on students' academic achievement and attitude	• Furnish support for data gathering and reporting about student achievement • Encourage qualitative methods of analyzing student attitude about the innovation
Stage 5: Collaboration	• Ready to share concerns • Prepared to collaborate with others to implement change	• Set up study/learning groups to plan and deliver implementation effectively • Include experienced teachers in professional development efforts
Stage 6: Refocusing	• Exploration of universal benefits from the innovation • Consideration of major change or replacement with a more powerful alternative	• Reinforce positive pedagogy that results from the innovation • Disseminate information about the widespread implementation of the innovation • Make provision for all interested voices to be heard • Support the change with appropriate resources

Figure 2.2

Figure 2.2 shows how these stages relate to both teachers facing the challenge of change (Individual Facing Change) and teacher-leaders who are helping lead change movements (Leading Change) as mentors, peer coaches, professional developers, curriculum or project directors.

Although each of the stages of concern are important, the sixth Stage of Concern, *Refocusing*, moves to systemic thinking and is a goal for teachers who would lead change. Stage Two, *Personal*, also generates systemic thinking on a personal level for those first encountering change because it necessitates thinking about the interrelated personal systems of beliefs, values, knowledge, skills, ethics, and actions that make up the whole person. Discounting an individual's personal concerns only causes defensiveness and resistance. A teacher-leader who is also a change agent respects the difficulty of change and recognizes the need for all the stakeholders affected by change to work through these stages of concerns as individuals and then as a community.

With the need for sensitivity to participants' stages of concern considered, the situations in which educational change occurs can be studied by those who wish to lead. Fullan (1993) explains that these change situations exhibit dynamic complexity because the causes and effects of a certain change are not always apparent, and appropriate action does not always produce expected outcomes. "Complexity, dynamism, and unpredictability, in other words, are not merely things that get in the way. They are normal" (Fullan 1993, 125). With this dynamic complexity in mind, Fullan specifies Eight Basic Lessons about the Process of Educational Change:

1. You can't mandate what matters.
2. Change is a journey, not a blueprint.
3. Problems are our friends.
4. Vision and strategic planning come later.
5. Individualism and collectivism must have equal power.
6. Neither centralization nor decentralization works.
7. Connection with the wider environment is critical for success.
8. Every person is a change agent.   (pp. 125–130)

Adapted from "Innovation, Reform, and Restructuring Strategies" by M. Fullan in *Challenges and Achievements of American Education*. © 1993 by the Association for Supervision and Curriculum Development, Alexandria, VA. Used with permission.

Fullan's Eight Basic Lessons about change offer a commonsense approach to dealing with the complexity that change entails. For example, policy makers can "mandate" standards to ensure quality and monitor performance. However, the more specifically leaders try to mandate educational goals, the more narrow the goals and means to achieve them become. What really matters for the implementation of change—skill level, creative thinking, and commitment to the change—cannot be mandated;

thinking cannot be forced; people cannot be made to change. Even the necessary skills and a commitment to change cannot ensure a successful outcome. Like qualitative research, it is impossible to know what will happen when the journey of change begins. Solutions for hypothetical problems or the impact of those solutions cannot be known in advance.

Developing suitable responses to complex situations demands the confrontation and solution of real problems that occur during change. This examination of problems allows the probing, retraining, and redesigning of unsuccessful programs. Successful schools have spent a great deal of time confronting their problems so that they might develop better coping strategies.

As schools seek to redesign and redefine themselves they often formulate a vision statement—a futuristic image of the organization—and then engage in strategic planning before any change is attempted. While the processes of systemic thinking and planning, integrative committees and work teams, and collaboration that strategic planning stresses are progressive and support change, Fullan asserts that vision should come later in the change process because people need reflective experiences before they can form a vision. A shared vision evolves over time through the interactions within a learning community, and skill development that supports the vision is essential. "The critical question should be how vision can be shaped and reshaped to make sense in the current situation" (Fullan 1993, 127).

Productive changes in a community of learners overcome the isolation of individual community members, but these changes should not promote mindless or forced thinking as a group. While the emphasis on learning communities encourages collaboration, collaboration itself is not always inherently good nor an individual's ideas inherently bad. Individual and group views need to be respected and pondered simultaneously so that decisions may reflect attention to the widest number of alternatives available.

Centralization (a top-down process) of decision making in schools may result in over control, but decentralization (a bottom-up process) may result in chaos and preoccupation with governance. Individual schools may achieve a highly collaborative culture, but they cannot stay highly collaborative all the time. "Key people leave, people get transferred, and so on. Two-way, top-down/bottom-up solutions are needed in which schools and districts influence each other through a continually-negotiated process and agenda" (Fullan 1993, 128).

The agenda that schools undertake must also recognize the community and state in which they reside by responding and contributing to the issues of the day. Leadership from the school-level should be a part of forming state policies, encouraging teacher learning, and seeking advice from both inside and outside the school. This wider view of school involvement in change issues is echoed by the call for involvement of all personnel within the school in change movements undertaken by the school.

Every person within an educational institution must be adept at managing change because no one person can possibly understand all the aspects of a schoolwide problem. A new organizational paradigm that involves all systems including faculty and staff within a school cannot be established by administrators acting alone. Teachers *are* change agents by their positioning within the school. Teacher-leaders are positive, proactive change agents because their REACH conduct compels them to seek the best for their students and their schools.

Teacher-leaders seeking to implement and sustain educational change as positive, proactive change agents can apply the following three-step process of analyzing, evaluating, executing to their decision making about change:

- **Analyzing:** Investigate the systemic nature of change—seek information about the patterns and relationships among all the systems in a school (personnel, curriculum, instruction, governance, assessment, professional development, personnel selection, and national/state/district standards and benchmarks, scheduling, technology, etc.).
- **Evaluating:** Recognize how a proposed change will affect these systems and their organization. Even change movements change and may need to be re-evaluated and redesigned to fit the current situation and modified goals.
- **Executing:** Act as change agents who move the task from one of forced or passive sharing to one of involvement and shared ownership—answering concerns, encouraging participation, and working together to formulate whole-system, long-term solutions.

STRATEGY FOR BECOMING A CHANGE AGENT

In his discussion of change and continuity in supervision and leadership Pajack (1993) states, "Schools are *teaching* organizations by definition, but are not necessarily *learning* organizations. Most schools are designed primarily to transmit information; in other words, they are not designed to generate or invent it" (p. 174). Yet, the future of education requires that schools learn, and that teacher-leaders within those schools see themselves as part of an interrelated learning, as well as teaching, system. In fact, Senge asserts that teachers as leaders are central to the process of establishing learning systems that "help people restructure their views of reality to see beyond the superficial conditions and events into the underlying causes of problems—and therefore to see new possibilities for shaping the future" (1990, 12).

Identifying conditions/problems and finding possibilities means change agents should analyze all aspects of change. One way to approach the study of change is with a Force Field Analysis. Designed by Lewin (1951) to analyze the state of balance between actions of opposing forces, Force Field

Analysis can be used by change agents to investigate factors that promote or inhibit change. Change is then empowered by adding helping forces and subtracting hindering forces. Hindering forces cannot be ignored, for as Schmuck reports, "they will defeat us, unless we work hard to reduce their power. Strive to create more facilitating forces, yes, but work even harder to put extra effort into decreasing the power of restraints" (1997, 11). Before this can happen, both helping and hindering forces must be identified. Figure 2.3 outlines the steps of a Force Field Analysis.

Force Field Analysis of Change ▶ ▶ ▶

1. Define the current change situation: _____

   _____

   _____

2. List the factors that help or hinder the change process:

   Change Situation:_____

   Factors That Help This Change   **Factors That Hinder This Change**

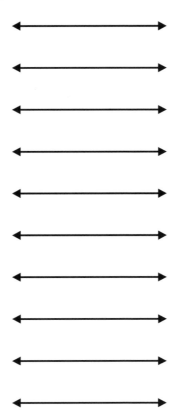

3. Seek consensus about the factors above.
4. Use different types of arrows (color or intensity) to indicate the groups' consensus about the impact of the factors.
5. Formulate a plan to effectively reinforce helping factors and to diminish the hindering forces.

Figure 2.3

TEACHERS AS CURRICULUM LEADERS

The Latin root of the word "curriculum" means racecourse. This is not meant to suggest that curriculum should be addressed or instructed at breakneck speed, but rather that it is meant to run a course, a circular process with a beginning and an end. The curricular process begins with suppositions about learners, identifies goals and benchmarks of those goals, organizes concepts within a scope and sequence, outlines procedures and learning environments, performs evaluation or assessment of the outcomes of those procedures, and begins again—learning from reflection and revising to reflect the learning. Inside school classrooms where the teacher is the natural leader, essential curricular questions tend to focus on the following:

> To be fond of learning is to be near the knowledge.
>
> Tze-sze

- What will be taught?
- In what instructional manner?
- With what results?
- With what resources?

The answers to these questions are clearly needed, but answers to questions that go deeper to a philosophical level that inform the essential questions are just as important:

- Why should this be taught?
- Who decides what is to be taught?
- How is this relevant to students' futures?
- How will this contribute to and sustain a learning community?

Approaching curricular decisions both from essential questions and the philosophical questions that inform them require that teachers possess expertise and skill levels that are constructed on a firm knowledge base. In addition, teachers' curricular decisions should reflect the significance of teaching and learning experiences within classrooms. The curricular involvement that results from daily connection with essential curricular questions and experiences also establishes the school as the logical unit for curricular improvements. Although district-level policy, support, and assessment is appropriate and necessary, Griffin states, "the work of curriculum change is logically the work of teachers and administrators in schools and classrooms" (1990, 195).

Curricular change is *not* the type of task relegated to a laborer and managed by an administrator; it is the kind of work shared by professionals who experience the daily activities within a school and are concerned about the future work and effectiveness of the school.

The idea of teacher-leaders participating actively in planning and curriculum decisions is supported by Connelly and Clandinin's definition of curriculum as "something experienced by people in situations" (1988, 6) and their theory that explains curriculum as experience.

Both tangible (instructional material or lack thereof, desks, computers—the overall physical environment) and intangible (instructional methods, personal interactions—everything that makes up the subtext of an environment) factors are part of the learning experience and are therefore integral parts of the curriculum. The "dynamic interaction" between tangible and intangible factors adds emotion and intensity to the notion of curriculum. This interaction reflects all of what has transpired in that classroom to that point, its history. It is this history that gives curriculum a depth and a past that needs to be considered when introducing change.

Designing for curricular change inevitably leads to planning future situations, giving curriculum a forward momentum or feel. Planning for future classroom situations often creates a type of anxiety because designers know that whatever they do is temporary and always in process. However, looking to the past and anticipating the future strengthens curriculum design because teacher-leaders are then working toward an end; they are setting up a situation that both teachers and students will experience. If curriculum design combines the experience of the situation with the past and the future, it can truly be celebrated as a meaningful inquiry process, not a dull, repetitive procedure that happens once a year and produces a curriculum guide that is as dry as it is pedantic.

What would it take to bring the curricular decisions made within a school to the level of work shared by professionals, the teacher-leaders who have direct experience with it? Moving curricular decisions to this level within a school system will require a comprehensive approach to the following three elements:

- Continued learning about curricular content and processes by teachers and administrators
- Collaborative methods of design that promote meaningful knowledge and connection among concepts
- Realistic plans about time, incentive, and connections for teachers as leaders of curriculum

This approach to curricular policy and design assumes risk-taking, knowledge, effectiveness, and autonomy from teacher-leaders. It also extends to them the opportunity to participate with colleagues in professional work that has real impact in the classroom and the obligation to make ethical curricular choices that teach social responsibility. Curricular leadership is the front line of teacher-leadership because of its connection to the classroom and student achievement. However, it also presents the challenge of dealing with time do curricular work for the classroom outside the classroom.

Time on task, allocated time, audited time, meeting time, mandated time, planning time, lunch time, release time—teachers are surrounded by issues of time. Yet there just doesn't seem to be enough. Beyond time actually spent in classroom instruction, teachers struggle with the lack of time to reflect, learn, and plan. How then can time be arranged to plan, design, implement, and assess curriculum? Time might be arranged so that teachers can be released for one teaching period on a series of days or arranging a period within the schedule for teams of teachers to meet at least twice a week. Team planning time can actually save individual teacher's planning time when the team uses their collaborative team time to talk about ideas, coordinate interdisciplinary curricular teaching/projects, and share technical skills among the group. Faculty meeting and professional development times can also include curricular issues.

Incentives for teacher-leaders who extend extra time and energy on creative and compelling curriculum can be tangible or symbolic. Griffin affirms that "it is increasingly apparent that teachers' conceptions of rewards are considerably more comprehensive and thoughtful than is sometimes believed" (1990, 202). Financial incentives are valued and stipends for extra work are justified, but teachers often find motivation in time release, help with routine paperwork, help from a teaching associate, or special recognition for curricular work.

The maxim that "many hands make the work lighter" recognizes that connections—resources, support, and colleagues—can help alleviate the crunch and burnout that any type of overwork can cause. School administrators can offer support by providing clerical help, technical support, and connections with curriculum experts and consultants. Universities and colleges also can provide resources and support through combined applied research projects and grant projects. The types of on-site resources available to teachers working with curriculum may be limited by the economic situation of a school district, but most teachers now have access to the Internet and World Wide Web where a wealth of resources wait. For example, the Association for Supervision and Curriculum Development (ASCD) offers a Web site called *Only the Best Web site* on which a curriculum leader would find over 3,000 pages of curricular material, including the ASCD Curriculum Handbook. Access to this site requires a paid subscription, but is worth the expenditure if only for the savings districts would realize by having access to the most current edition of the organization's curriculum handbook. Also found on the Web are discipline-specific Internet sites that offer free resources, lesson activities, and assessment ideas.

Curricular teacher-leaders tend to go into education because they enjoyed school and still enjoy learning. Yet too often they function as isolated individuals, and their intellectual growth is not sustained by the very educational institutions for which they work. As Poplin asserts, "A strong ethic of collective study can provide for the commonalties and differences in the way humans grow and counter the intellectual starvation many teachers feel" (1992, 11). Involving teacher-leaders in the study, development, implementation, and critique of curriculum can stimulate their continued growth and increase the likelihood of the success of curriculum reform, which is specific to the context of the school and the needs of its students.

STRATEGY FOR BECOMING A CURRICULUM LEADER

Wiggins and McTighe (1998) begin their book, *Understanding by Design*, by describing teachers as design professionals who create learning experiences to meet specific needs. They go on to say, "We are also designers of assessments to diagnose students' needs to guide our teaching and to enable us, our students, and others (parents and administrators) to determine whether our goals have been achieved; that is, did the students learn and understand the desired knowledge?" (Wiggins and McTighe 1998, 7)

Like other design professionals (architects, engineers, etc.), teachers have standards as well as learner considerations that provide a framework for curriculum development. When these standards and considerations are the foundation of the goals of classroom instruction or the end product, the curriculum becomes the means to that end. Unlike most curriculum developed by teachers that start with a text or activity, this strategy suggests that teachers as curriculum leaders should design curriculum backwards, beginning with the end in mind.

There are three stages in a backward design process:

1. Stage One—Identify desired results.
2. Stage Two—Determine acceptable evidence.
3. Stage Three—Plan learning experiences and instruction.

Adapted from *Understanding by Design* by G. Wiggins and J. McTighe. © 1998 by the Association for Supervision and Curriculum Development, Alexandria, VA. Used with permission.

In Stage One, goals, national/state/district standards, and district expectations are used to make decisions about what knowledge, skills, assessments, and big ideas should be included in the a unit. In Stage Two, teachers make decisions about how students can demonstrate what they know and can do. Such demonstrations can take the form of a variety of assessments, both formal and informal, which take place throughout the unit. The planning at this stage, however, is meant to identify what types of evidence are best suited to demonstrate the knowledge or skill identified in Stage One. Stage Three begins with thinking carefully about the essential knowledge and skills students will need to know, then what activities, methods, resources, and materials are necessary to achieve understanding of that knowledge and those skills. Because assessment is an integral part of instruction, this stage would also be the place to clarify and pinpoint criteria for assessment so that it reflects the type of instruction used.

Using a backward design may involve a different type of movement through a textbook because it identifies and plans for essential learnings that may not occur in the chronological fashion of many textbooks. This type of design is especially effective for interdisciplinary planning based on a common theme because the first step in the design process that identifies goals, standards, and expectations would include decisions about the theme. Using the Curriculum Design for a Teaching and Learning Unit that follows as a guide, teacher-leaders can formulate a backward design of a unit they would be interested in developing as a curriculum leader.

Curriculum Design for a Teaching and Learning Unit ▶ ▶ ▶

STAGE 1 - WHAT ARE THE DESIRED RESULTS?

Essential Content Standards: (What is the lasting benefit to students?)

State Standards: (Which state standards will I meet in this unit?)

Benchmarks: (What do students need to know and be able to do?)

Technology Integration: (Is technology infusion appropriate to this unit? If so, how will it be used?)

STAGE 2 - WHAT IS THE ACCEPTABLE EVIDENCE OF LEARNING?

Specific Evidence of Student Learning: (Test data, projects, portfolios, etc.)

Types of Assessment: (How will I measure what students know and are able to do?)

STAGE 3 - WHAT LEARNING EXPERIENCES, RESOURCES, AND INSTRUCTION WILL BE USED?

Experiences and Instructional Strategies: (How will I design learning opportunities that enable ALL students to be successful? What materials and resources do I need?)

TEACHERS AS SITUATIONAL LEADERS

> Leaders teach. Teaching and leading are distinguishable occupations, but every great leader is clearly teaching—and every great teacher is leading.
>
> —JOHN GARDNER

Do teachers really want to be leaders and make their own decisions? According to Foster, "Folk wisdom among principals has it that the superstars do indeed want to have an impact on their professional lives, but the average teacher—perhaps 95 percent—just want someone to tell them what to do" (1990, 38). This type of folk wisdom has at its root the myth that there are natural leaders, born leaders, who are more fit to make decisions than the followers they command. But every person may be a leader in some situations and a follower in others. Cooperative learning strategies have demonstrated the strength of a leadership approach where leadership roles vary according to the task, and leaders vary their approaches according to the group.

Situational Leadership

A situational leader is any member of a group that furthers the goals of the group and contributes to its growth, influencing task performance and satisfaction of the group members (such as an active member of a school textbook committee). This type of leadership is circular in practice because all members of a group have the potential for leadership in any given situation, and the situational leader's style varies with the situation and the group. For situational leadership to be effective, a group leader may choose to emphasize an assigned task, deal with group members' concerns, or both. It all depends on what the group needs to be successful.

Because situational leadership is usually earned by task expertise and directed toward the function of the group, it is generally more accepted by the group as long as it is appropriate. For example, a facilitative leadership style may be appropriate with experienced teachers who know one another, but a more cooperative problem-solving leader may be needed with a group that has never worked together.

The problem-solving type of situational leadership is an adaptation of a democratic style wherein the leader assumes a "team leader" position. Besides working cooperatively with the group to form goals and solve problems collaboratively, this situational leader works hard to create a humanistic environment of mutual respect, responsibility, and reciprocal influence. This leadership situation does not ignore personalities, but tries to meet both the needs of the group and its individual members. It also encourages ownership and pride in a project, which in turn, ensures the support of the team for the implementation of the project.

The Path-Goal Theory of Situational Leadership, developed by House and Mitchell (1981), directs situational leaders to match the interpersonal or situational variables of group characteristics and task difficulty with four types of leadership approaches: directive, supportive, achievement-oriented, and participative. Each leadership approach as well as group characteristics and task difficulty associated with that leadership approach in the Path-Goal Theory is outlined in Figure 2.4.

Leadership Approach of the Path-Goal Theory

Leadership Approach	Group Characteristics	Task Difficulty
Directive	Members like directions.	Task is unstructured.
Supportive	Members like freedom.	Task is already structured.
Achievement-Oriented	Members clearly understand paths to the goal.	Task is motivational and satisfying.
Participative	Members like an interpersonal approach.	Tasks are tied to rewards.

Figure 2.4

A teacher-leader following House and Mitchell's theory would choose the type of leadership behavior the group with whom they were working and adjust that behavior as the situation warranted.

The advantages of situational leadership are numerous because it fosters the behaviors that are characteristic of teacher-leadership:

- Creativity as part of risk-taking
- Participation and communication as part of effectiveness
- Trust, recognition, and support as part of autonomy
- Collaboration as part of collegiality
- Ethical modeling as part of honor

Situational leadership does, however take time and may not produce a clear, consistent direction. As educators move toward the goal of shared leadership, the question to be considered is not only what type of leader is best for the group in a given situation, but what level of situational leadership is needed from all the group members to best complete the task.

STRATEGY FOR BECOMING A SITUATIONAL LEADER

Working with groups (students, administrators, teachers, staff) within a school or with those groups that bring pressure from outside schools (parents, community groups, state departments of education, etc.) may demand different approaches, but they all involve personal relationships. To establish order in situational leadership and make wise decisions about relationships with a variety of groups, Bolman and Deal (1994) suggest that teachers use the perceptions by which they define and frame reality inside and outside the classroom. These perceptions, or frames of reality, are ways of viewing a situation that actually determines the type of leadership action one will employ in a given situation. "Even if your lenses or frames are sometimes off target, you still have to use them, because they give order to confusion and let you act rather than lapse into paralysis" (Bolman and Deal 1994, 4).

Multiple frames of leadership function like a variety of instructional models for teachers; they are conscious efforts to size up a situation from different perspectives. Each frame is used for a particular type of approach, but having multiple frames gives the teacher-leader a choice of approaches and allows re-framing or reorganizing if the first approach does not seem to be productive. Bolman and Deal have outlined four frames that are helpful in responding to school situations (see Figure 2.5).

Four Frames of Leadership

1. **The Human Resource Frame**—highlights the importance of needs and motives.
2. **The Political Frame**—points out the limits of authority and the scarcity of resources.
3. **Structural Frame**—emphasizes productivity, coordinated authority, policies, and clear rules.
4. **Symbolic Frame**—centers attention on symbols, meaning, belief, and faith. Symbols can govern informally through implicit rules, shared values, and common understandings.

Adapted from *Becoming a Teacher Leader: From Isolation to Collaboration* by L. G. Bolman and T. E. Deal. © 1994 by Corwin Press, Thousand Oaks, CA. Used with permission.

Figure 2.5

The Human Resource Frame concentrates on relationship building and satisfying needs in a caring, trusting work environment. This frame supports leadership activities by opening up the lines of communication by conveying a sense of caring and respect, asking questions and listening, encouraging feedback, and stressing honesty in communication and relationships. This is the frame to use when one needs to build relationships among the group or with other groups.

The Political Frame maps the politics of the situation for a leader. Within this frame, key questions emerge: Who are the key players? What are their interests? How much power does each player have? Based on answers to these questions, you would be able to clarify agendas, build alliances, deal openly with conflict, and negotiate a solution. While political divisions within a school can be troublesome, they can also be a source of energy and renewal.

The Structural Frame works best when rules are explicit and are followed by everyone. Within this frame, you would clarify your role within the group, clarify policy to avoid conflict, and design groups for success by making sure that the goal and processes for reaching it are absolutely clear.

The Symbolic Frame celebrates values and common culture among the group. To be effective within this frame, a leader would need to learn the history of the group, diagnose the strength of the existing culture, identify the cultural players, reinforce and celebrate the culture's strength. Celebration among teachers and administrators about their common educational experiences does not happen frequently. It must be planned to create a shared sense of meaning and commitment.

Situational Leadership Strategy ▷ ▶ ▶

Teachers chosen to work with administrators to implement a new program might use the frames below to project a number of approaches to meet their goal. This chart uses each of Bolman and Deal's frames of leadership to describe strategies one might employ to help implement a new program or implement changes to an existing program.

Frames of Leadership Applied to Crisis Response

Human Resource Frame	Political Frame
Structural Frame	Symbolic Frame

Bolman and Deal's First Law of Holes: "When you're in one, stop digging!" (1994, 22)

TEACHERS AS TRANSFORMATIONAL LEADERS

Teacher-leadership in action should be just that—leading the group to action and leading the action toward a goal. Such movements may be subtle, effecting small changes by working toward a goal slowly. Other movements, however, may call for more drastic measures; those movements may even seek to transform an entire organizational culture. Transformational movements that necessitate such drastic measures require the combined, extraordinary effort of teachers and administrators who are willing to build and transform leadership altogether. Members of such a leadership team by necessity come to share goals and visions, which in turn bind them in a moral commitment to proactive change. Schlechty issues a call for this exceptional type of leadership: "What the reinvention of American education calls for—just as the reinvention of other institutions in America requires—are transformational leaders: people who can create visions and goals that cause men and women to transform the institutions of which they are part" (1990, 151).

> The future belongs to those who believe in the beauty of their dreams.
> —ELEANOR ROOSEVELT

Transformational leadership, like situational leadership, recognizes the need to see purpose and significance in individual and group actions. But this level of leadership goes beyond situational leadership by providing the inspiration for performance beyond general expectations and incentives for personal and group improvement. Once the needs and concerns of individuals are supported, transformational leaders can work on sustaining performance and building momentum within school improvement endeavors by seeking a shared vision that provides a point of focus for the entire school. Within transformational leadership, "a new kind of hierarchy emerges in the school—one that places purposes, values, and commitments at the apex and teachers, principals, parents, and students below in service to these purposes" (Sergiovanni 1990, 27).

To begin the challenging task of transformation, DuBrin (1995) indicates that teacher-leaders should take the following actions:

1. **Raise people's awareness.** The transformational leader helps group members equate personal pride and financial rewards with the achievement of the organization's goals. He or she also informs group members about the criteria necessary to meet those goals.

2. **Help people look beyond self-interest.** Beyond personal financial rewards, the transformational leader helps group members understand how achieving the organization's goals strengthens the organization of which they are a part, giving them a stronger professional base.

3. **Help people search for self-fulfillment.** The transformational leader helps people see beyond the small benefits to focus on a vision of an improved and self-fulfilled future.

4. **Help people understand the need for change.** The transformational leader helps group members deal with change both emotionally

and intellectually. Any change involves new patterns and challenges that naturally evoke emotional responses and intellectual tasks. Group members need opportunities to discuss and understand the need for change.

5. **Invest managers with a sense of urgency.** To create the transformation, the leader assembles a supportive group of managers and challenges to meet the demands of change by sharing a vision that is credible and achievable.

6. **Commit to greatness.** By adopting this greatness attitude, leaders can honor human nature and strengthen social structures. An emphasis on ethical leadership within transformation, however, requires quality and service, which are just as important to the process and product of change as are involvement and feelings of ownership. (1995, 69–70)

Adapted from *Leadership: Research Findings, Practice, and Skills* by A. J. DuBrin. © 1995 by Houghton Mifflin Co., Boston. Reprinted with permission.

With the hierarchical administrative structure so firmly entrenched in public education, can transformational leadership really work? Such restructuring may be viewed through the experience of businesses that began a shift from Type A organizations to Type Z organizations in the 1980's. A Type A organization is one based on competition and top-down power. This type of power controls decisions about personnel, resources, and professional development. A Type Z organization, on the other hand, uses members of the organization as much as possible for decision making. The type of power exercised in an ideal organization is *facilitative* power— power activated *through* other people, not *over* other people. Such power arises in education when "teachers are helped to find greater meaning in their work, to meet higher-level needs through their work, and to develop enhanced instructional capacities" (Leithwood 1992, 9).

Substantial research confirms that when businesses shift organization, power, and leadership, they have experienced greater productivity. Studies involving transformational leadership in educational settings have been limited, but those that have been completed (Deal and Peterson 1990; Leithwood and Jantzi 1991) indicate a positive influence on teacher collaboration and teacher change in attitude and practice.

During his investigation of the effects of transformational leadership in education, Leithwood found school cultures that were responsive to this type of leadership. He observed that such schools were involved in a continuing quest for three major objectives (Leihwood 1992, 9–10):

1. To help staff members develop and maintain a collaborative, professional school culture
2. To foster teacher development
3. To help teachers solve problems together more effectively

Change within schools is not quick and results take years to achieve. Mitchell and Tucker suggest that "it is time to recognize that leadership is less a matter of aggressive action than a way of thinking and feeling— about ourselves, about our jobs, and about the nature of the educational process" (1992, 30). Changing thinking about the jobs that educators perform in light of the larger notion of an educational vision makes cooperative participation among all members of an educational culture possible and the cumulative power of the organization unlimited.

STRATEGY FOR BECOMING A TRANSFORMATIONAL LEADER

In ancient Greece, pilgrims traveled great distances to the southern slopes of Mount Parnasus to consult the famous Delphi Oracle. The Oracle, housed at the Temple of Apollo that Greeks designated as the center of the earth, was thought to have great powers of divine prophecy. The visions imparted by the Oracle were given in such ambiguous ways that they could generally be interpreted as true, and could seldom be proven wrong. Transformational teacher-leaders today are certainly not expected to be divine, but they too should be able to help define the educational vision or destination for the future of their schools that could generally be interpreted as true.

Within an organization, Bennis and Nanus have defined a vision as "a view of a realistic, credible, attractive future for the organization, a condition that is better in some important ways than what now exists" (1985, 89). From this perspective, a vision is not some fuzzy, ambiguous prophecy delivered annually to the School Board, but a concrete statement of purpose that requires analysis of a school's values. All schools share the value of student learning, and it is at this center that vision statements must begin. What is the school's vision of a graduate? What should students know and be able to do when they graduate? The values of the school community are clearly a part of the hypothetical student graduate who is the embodiment of the vision. For example, a graduate who is able to think critically, act responsibly, appreciate diverse cultures, work collaboratively, communicate effectively, seek and use knowledge well, solve problems efficiently, and model technological literacy is truly a student exemplar.

Making a school vision realistic, credible, and part of an attractive future, however, requires the involvement of the entire learning community in going beyond the nature of the graduate to the further analysis of the school organization and its operation. What is the learning community's vision of an excellent teaching/learning environment? What is the school's approach to teaching/learning? What would it take to produce the "visionary" student? What is a possible and desirable future state of the school? How can the desirable state of the school be attained? What is the desirable future state for education in general?

Clearly formulating a school vision for transformation is no longer the right or responsibility of a single administrator. Creating a school vision is a collaborative process that depends on teacher-leaders to use the REACH characteristics of conduct while contributing to and implementing a school vision for transformation as illustrated in the table below.

Creating a School Vision for Transformation

REACH Behaviors	Process of Formulating a School Vision
Risk-Taking	Think Futuristic.
Effectiveness	Be concrete and knowledgeable in defining the outcomes for a graduate who embodies the vision.
Autonomy	Act out the vision in your own classroom.
Collegiality	Communicate with others about the vision and share the excitement of the vision.
Honor	Choose outcomes with worthy values that speak to the education of the mind as well as the social responsibility of future citizens.

Figure 2.7

A Teacher-Leader's Vision of Transformation

With the REACH behaviors guiding their process, teacher-leaders can envision, think, and write about their vision for the ideal graduate and school using the following questions. Like a professional philosophy, outlining a vision is the first step in making it happen.

How might one envision the Ideal Graduate?

List what students should know and be able to do when they graduate below:

How might you envision an excellent teaching/learning environment?

What is the desirable future state for education in general?

Looking Back/REACHing Forward ▶ ▶ ▶

This chapter began with a discussion of teachers as change agents. If the role of the teacher as a change agent were placed in the center of a series of concentric circles, you could trace the development of leadership roles and experiences outward through curriculum design and practice, specific situations, and then as a member of a transformational leadership community, as illustrated in the diagram below.

Teacher-Leadership in Action

What have been your experiences at each of these levels?

How would your present position be altered if you participated as a teacher-leader at each of these levels?

Teachers-Leaders and Professional Growth and Development

▶   ▶   ▶   ▶   ▶   ▶   ▶   ▶   ▶   ▶

Educational change and the execution of new ideas on site at the school level necessitate both learning and leadership by the educators at that site. Biologically, the concept of growth indicates an increase in size, while development represents an increase or change in function. Educationally, growth denotes an increase in knowledge or skills that require learning. Development, on the other hand, suggests the internalization and application of knowledge or skills. Development calls for both learning and leadership.

Because the context or culture of a school site often determines how teachers perceive, accept, prepare for, and accomplish change, professional growth and development work best in a supportive context. Effective change needs individual commitment, but it also calls for organizational review and retooling of schools to support that change. The success or failure of novice teachers depends on the school in which they teach. Conversely, the better the teachers within the school, the better the school. Fullan emphasizes teachers' impact on schools when he reports, "continuous development of all teachers is the cornerstone for meaning, improvement, and reform" (1991, 315).

It is clear that in a collaborative learning and teaching environment, there can be no passive agents of change. As teachers develop the knowledge and confidence to see themselves as professionals capable of leading teaching and learning, the institution becomes a school improvement laboratory, especially tailored for learners at all levels. Inside that laboratory, professional development may be undertaken so that a specific change is successful, but it cannot flourish as a unique event or a one-shot inservice. Professional development must be imbedded in normative, professional reviews and learning, a part of being a teacher-leader. Accordingly, professional development is an element of teacher-leadership that is informed by the professional roles teachers undertake in their classrooms and schools, but looks to REACH behaviors as its base (see model in Figure 3.1).

The REACH Model

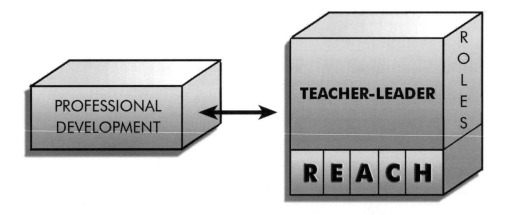

Figure 3.1

PROFESSIONAL GROWTH AND DEVELOPMENT

> Growth itself contains the germ of happiness
> —PEARL BUCK

Traditionally, the definition of a professional rested in the type of work one did and the commitment, preparation, power, and control one exhibited. From this it can be assumed that a professional engages in work that demands specialized qualifications and practice. Professional qualifications usually translate into advanced, rigorous education and the development of expertise needed to practice successfully within that profession. Professional work also suggests a calling or commitment to one's work beyond the general parameters of a job. A committed professional is able to both describe and defend her or his beliefs and approach, engage in critical reflection, assess the results of his or her work, and revise practice based upon this cycle of inquiry. In other words, a professional knows what she or he is doing and is able to *profess* that knowledge as well as the philosophy and research that informs it. Finally, professionals monitor the quality of their profession by establishing entrance requirements and developing peer review procedures.

Since the 1960s, debate about teachers' status as professionals has centered around measuring their work and responsibilities against that of the legal and medical professions. Are teachers professionals, semiprofessionals, or skilled workers? As part of analyzing selected professional occupations including educators, architects, engineers, physicians, nurses, law-related occupations, accountants, and social workers, Rowan in cooperation with the U.S. Department of Education rated the complexity of teachers' work. Rowan found that the professional status of teaching cannot markedly change without longer preparation and quality controls exerted by teachers themselves. However, he also found that "teaching children and adolescents is complex work, and successful performance of this work requires high levels of general educational development and specific vocational preparation" (Rowan 1994, 13). Current efforts that expect and encourage teachers to develop their own and their students' capabilities as part of their professionalism are aimed at the right target. Education, after all, is not about development as an endeavor on Wednesday afternoons twice a month. Education is the development of the self, the development of the community.

In a different approach to the question of teacher professionalism, Barone et al. offer a perspective that defines a professional teacher in the context of the education occupation itself, not other occupations. They have identified three dimensions critical to evaluating teaching as its own profession: the articulative, operational, and political dimensions (Barone et al. 1996, 1111).

Articulative Dimensions of Teaching

Through critical reflection, strong professionals can articulate what they consider effective and meaningful in their teaching and learning. They make informed and data-driven decisions about educational processes and curriculum. They are able to recognize essential questions and to generate their own probing questions as well as describe their own educational identities—their professional selves. The ability to reflect critically, to communicate knowledge, to question, and to generate a professional identify supports teacher-leadership by employing all the REACH behaviors that define leadership.

Operational Dimension of Teaching

The operational dimension of strong professional teachers requires that they function or operate in congruence with the philosophy and pedagogy they articulate. "Neither technical skill nor deep affection for a particular planning or teaching approach will, alone, suffice for the operational dimension of strong professionalism." (Barone et al. 1996, 1113). There is also the requirement that teachers be allowed to operate professionally.

Professionalism is denied when mandated methodologies or assessments are incompatible with a teacher's well-informed curriculum design and the needs of his or her students.

The Political Dimension of Teaching

This dimension of professionalism concerns the political efforts of teachers to establish the opportunity and respect to implement curriculum they deem effective and meaningful within their respective classrooms. This element differentiates between *profession-alism*, which focuses on service to others and *profession-ism*, which serves to restrict and mystify membership within an occupation. Professional teachers realize that power should be shared democratically, and they model a code of ethics that focuses on the interests of their students. This may mean that teachers need to introduce needed change and educate others about educational constraints that interfere with the operation or practice of the beliefs and values they have articulated. Teacher-leaders, then, seek to develop and demonstrate professionalism so they may positively impact their students' lives and learning.

STRATEGY FOR DEVELOPING A PHILOSOPHY OF PROFESSIONALISM

Learning approaches that embrace cognitive and brain-based theories are as appropriate for teachers as the traditional K-12 students they serve. Outdated staff development programs, which attempt to "fix" all teachers in all disciplines at all levels with a stand-alone workshop, typically ignore what is known about how to accelerate learning. To accelerate learning, professional development workshops should do the following:

- provide a choice and a variety of teaching models to its participants.
- engage the emotions.
- offer a sensory-rich environment.
- connect with previous learning.
- employ active learning strategies.

Each step above actively engages the teacher-leader as a learner. Licklider contends that an interaction between the material and the teacher-learner is vital for ownership and acceptance of professional growth and development, "failure to embrace education as a true profession in which practitioners have an obligation for their own continuing professional growth has contributed to the failure of staff development programs" (1997, 38).

The following self-reflective strategy introduces a method of clarifying and solidifying one's own philosophy of professionalism so that those tenets become part of a teacher-leader's self-description and self-direction as a leader and learner. Teachers can reflect upon the three dimensions of educational professionalism discussed above—articulative, operational, and political—in terms of the following critical questions offered by Licklider in order to refine and more adequately represent one's educational beliefs.

1. *What is the assumption* (content of a concept)?
2. *How did I come to hold that assumption* (process of a concept)?
3. *Why does this assumption matter* (premise of a concept)?

(1997, 39)

This critical reflection about how one defines his or her professional identity through self-knowledge is an important step in addressing the Effectiveness and Autonomy behaviors of the REACH model. Professional development for teacher-leaders should evolve from what those teachers and their students are doing in the classroom, and what they need to be doing in the future. As professional teachers and leaders approach such a future, Talbert and McLaughlin reiterate the importance of development: "Without opportunities to acquire new knowledge, to reflect on practice, and to share successes and failures with colleagues, teachers are not likely to develop a sense of professional control and responsibility" (1994, 130).

Philosophy of an Educational Professional ▶ ▶ ▶

After careful self-reflection, teachers can use the questions below to refine or create their own professional educational philosophy. Organizing reflections in a matrix supplies information about and clarifies relationships among those reflections.

Dimensions of Education Professionalism

What is your view?

How did you come to hold this view?

Why does it matter?

Articulative

▶ What is the role of education?

▶ What is the role of teachers in student learning?

▶ What is the role of students in their learning?

Operation

▶ How do your classroom practices exemplify the beliefs and values you have articulated above?

Political

▶ How do you create professional oppportunities to implement the activities you identified above as important?

MODELS OF PROFESSIONAL DEVELOPMENT

Professional development for teacher-leaders involves elements common to any successful adult education program—involvement, participation, ownership, and relevance. Although it is vital to have a consensus about school improvement goals within a learning community, part of acknowledging teachers as adults, leaders, and professionals is giving them choices about how they will achieve those goals. In making a choice for professional development, teachers may choose individual routes, or school communities may choose an approach that works for the task and the group. Accordingly, Sparks and Loucks-Horsley (1989) suggest five approaches to professional development that involve reflection at some level and have been proven effective:

1. Training-Coaching Model
2. Self-Directed Development Model
3. School Improvement Process Model
4. Action Research Model
5. Classroom-Based Development Model

> Training is everything. The peach was once a bitter almond; cauliflower is nothing but a cabbage with a college education.
>
> —MARK TWAIN

The Training-Coaching Model

The Training-Coaching Model works best when it is imperative to deliver information quickly, develop technical skills, or present new information at the awareness level. This model is cost effective and most efficient with large groups. Originally designed to expand a teacher's repertoire of skills or techniques, the training-coaching model has adjusted to results-driven professional development movements by focusing on student outcomes and the improvement of teacher thinking. The Training-Coaching Model of professional development "has shown consistent results when training content can be represented as a repertoire of discrete practices and where classroom performance is oriented toward specified student outcomes" (Little 1994, 159). For example, packaged training programs from national organizations often offer strong training in specific skills. Applying the Training-Coaching Model in this manner, however, is limited because a standardized package lacks responsiveness to the unique needs of a school community if it does not include follow-up and coaching within the workplace. Packaged training also places teachers in a passive role, receiving information as consumers and technicians instead of producers and designers of that information. The Training-Coaching Model is beneficial to teacher-leaders in that it offers information and builds skills. The benefits of this model, however, are often offset by the lack of individual autonomy and relevance for classroom teachers-leaders.

Self-Directed Development Model

The Self-Directed Development Model involves independent study of a teaching skill or area of knowledge directed toward the achievement of students. This does not necessarily mean that a teacher who elects individually-guided development needs to be isolated. Small groups of teachers who are independently studying a topic or trying a new strategy may cluster together periodically to discuss their progress and concerns. Although student achievement is the focus, this model takes full advantage of job-embedded development and respects the adult as a special type of learner. Sparks and Hirsh report that job-embedded learning links new knowledge to present and authentic problems: "It is based on the assumption that the most powerful learning is that which occurs in response to challenges currently being faced by the learner and that allows for immediate application, experimentation, and adaptation on the job" (1997, 52). In the future, experts anticipate that job-embedded strategies will increase, giving on-site educators a chance to organize, lead, and share information and practice.

Independent study can yield experience-based knowledge and practice that enriches cognitive growth and confidence. It also has a positive effect on one's teaching and problem-solving abilities. When engaged in reflection and problem solving, adults also seem to develop a dialectical, or deductive, form of thinking. "Not only are adult dialectical thinkers more sensitive to contradictions—and more tolerant of them—but they have also learned a series of procedures for dealing with them" (LeFrancois 1990, 591). Adults who think deductively have the ability to reason about complex systems that elude and frustrate younger learners (and sometimes younger teachers) and enjoy their greatest period of creativity during middle age.

As adult learners and leaders, many teachers do have the capability to design their own development. When this development is voluntary and chosen by the individual, it has the dual advantages of having intrinsic motivation and meeting unique needs in specific classrooms. Most teachers are active, strong, and diverse learners who can focus their needs and design their development. Figure 3.2 the "Self-Directed Development Process" provides a framework teachers can use to design such a plan.

School Improvement Process Model

Within a School Improvement Process Model, teachers collaborate as partners with administrative staff and/or consultants to establish programs that produce improved student outcomes, organizational development, and professional development of the participants. While efforts may take the form of grant writing, curriculum design, or work with other teachers or consultants in classroom practice, teachers' development within this model falls under the umbrella of school improvement.

Self-Directed Development Process

1. Use the completed Philosophy of an Educational Professional page to reflect about your beliefs, values, and pedagogical approaches.

2. Prioritize your professional needs with a Force Field Analysis (see chapter 2). What needs have to be addressed immediately? What educational development do you need to activate your professional philosophy?

3. Make a one-year plan outlining your goals for an entire school year, addressing immediate needs. Then formulate a three-year plan to help you further extend your professional goal planning.

4. Begin with your strongest interest or need and translate that goal into realistic action steps.

5. Look for support from colleagues, staff, and administrators. Schools often have hidden pockets of expertise in their staff. Finding and using support from within can also create relationships based on shared interests.

6. Celebrate your success and progress as you continue to grow and develop.

Figure 3.2

This model invites teachers within a particular school to share their common interests and needs in the context of their own school setting. The collaborative nature of this endeavor provides the opportunity for all staff members to engage in reflective teaching, goal setting, creative problem-solving, and assessment of a school improvement plan. Because the development needs are crosscurricular with a schoolwide impact, the context of this model is inclusive, building community and combating isolation. In addition, Feimen-Nemser and Floden suggest that shared professional development may also facilitate cooperative types of teaching: "The relationship of teaching cultures to the social systems of school, community, and society makes a multidisciplinary approach to learning particularly fruitful" (1990, 523).

Like the other professional development models presented here, the School Improvement Process Model has student achievement as its major outcome, so each step in the professional development process is a step toward accomplishing the overall goal of school improvement. The sequential nature of a long-term improvement plan, however, requires time—time to study the research relevant to the school improvement goals and to discuss application in a specific school setting, time to assimilate and to respond, and time to assess and to adapt.

The Action Research Model

The Action Research Model involves teacher-directed, classroom research on-site. Teachers set goals, formulate questions about their own practice, collect and analyze data, and find answers in a cycle of applied or action research. When teacher-leaders practice action research, they are able to apply their findings immediately, create rationale or professional space for current practices, or see practices in new ways. Schmuck defines action research as a planned inquiry, a search of information and answers: "It consists of both self-reflective inquiry, which is internal and subjective, and inquiry-oriented practice, which is external and data based. Action research is a sort of formal investigation into oneself or into one's own social system "(1997, 28–29).

While action research cannot be generalized in the same way as "pure" research can, it provides the data and insight to study and improve the work of the teacher/researcher, to answer a research question specific to a teacher-leader's classroom. For example, an elementary teacher may be interested in researching a particular approach to reading while a secondary teacher may be interested in researching student motivation strategies. Beyond providing answers to authentic classroom problems, action research supports REACH behaviors by strengthening teachers' intellectual functioning and self-assurance as they actively construct knowledge about teaching and learning. Cochran-Smith and Lytle argue that "teacher researchers are uniquely positioned to provide a truly emic, or insider's, perspective that makes visible the ways that students and teachers together construct knowledge and curriculum" (1993, 43). The reflective thinking and informed action that the Action Research Model prompts clearly links teaching and learning with knowing and understanding—the intent of professional development.

The Classroom-Based Development Model

The Classroom-Based Development Model employs observation and feedback to improve teaching. Professional development begins with teacher practice, which is best analyzed within its natural setting. Feedback provided by a peer without evaluative weight is a powerful way for teachers to learn and to share. Moreover, the successful exercise of the Classroom-Based Development Model both helps participants identify clear goals and enjoy support while working on those goals.

Attainment of a set of individual goals involves personal change, so it can be threatening. However, peer coaching, cognitive coaching, and mentoring allow staff members to work individually and cooperatively toward meeting those goals. Peer coaching removes both the isolation of working alone and the perceived threat of having a year's work evaluated in one or two one-hour visits by an administrator. Ideally, all educators in a school would see themselves as coaches or mentors for one another, providing companionship, sharing knowledge, and participating in decisions and problem solving.

By observing and coaching, team members become sensitized to their own teaching behaviors; they have a chance to discuss general issues of teaching and learning together, and they are able to observe a variety of teaching styles. As team members working toward a goal, these teachers are also active learners and have taken a large step toward becoming autonomous leaders.

Professional development for the complex set of individuals who make up a school community has many levels that require a variety of strategies. Traditionally, development has been organized by administrators and often conducted by experts who visit the school to provide training. Advances in cognitive and adult learning theory as well as the growing realization of the importance of teachers as leaders has led to a different concept of professional development—one in which the responsibility for development has been spread throughout the school system. School improvement demands both organizational change and individual change. Working in professional development to produce positive change offers exciting new roles for professional teachers who are prepared to lead.

STRATEGIES FOR WORKING WITH MODELS OF PROFESSIONAL DEVELOPMENT

Job-embedded and teacher-led professional development encourages individual ownership and acceptance of change. This type of development also encourages collegiality and cooperation by acknowledging that teachers are also resources for one another. One of the most important ways of extending and expanding those human resources is through the critical thinking skills central to inquiry and discovery. All of the models for professional development described in this chapter benefit from critical inquiry; most require it. Although the inquiry process can be completed individually, it does not have to be undertaken alone. Teachers' minds and their classroom questions do not exist in a social vacuum. Sharing ideas, perceptions, interpretations, and tentative solutions makes everyone stronger.

> Let us, each to the other, be a Gift as is the Buffalo. Let us teach each other.
> —HYEMEYOSHSTS STORM

The end result of critical inquiry is problem-solving and decision-making, the tools of leadership. The strategy provided here, however, looks at the entire inquiry cycle, exploring the variety of thinking skills that are engaged throughout the process so that any inquiry can be constructed and completed appropriately. The Inquiry Cycle basically revolves around generating ideas, designing ways to test those ideas, evaluating and analyzing the results of the testing, and making adjustments as the cycle begins again. That cycle would not be possible, however, without using the critical thinking skills involved at the various stages of the process. The stages of the inquiry cycle integrated with critical thinking skills as outlined by Callahan et al. (1998, 261) are shown in Figure 3.3.

Inquiry Process Integrated with Thinking Skills

Stages of the Inquiry Process	Thinking Skills by Stage
Stage 1 Generating ideas:	Thinking skills: explaining, generating, inferring, interpreting data, making analogies, synthesizing
Stage 2 Designing ways to test ideas	Thinking skills: applying controlling variables, defining operationally, hypothesizing, model building, predicting
Stage 3 Testing the idea	Thinking skills: communicating, experiencing, measuring, observing, verifying
Stage 4 Interpreting the results	Thinking skills: charting and graphing, classifying, comparing, ordering, sequencing, using numbers

Adapted from *Teaching in the Middle and Secondary Schools* by J. F. Callahan et al. © 1998 by Prentice Hall, Inc., Upper Saddle River, N.J. Reprinted with permission.

Figure 3.3

Teachers can use the Critical Inquiry Map that follows to contemplate any critical inquiry and identify what type of thinking will be needed to process and complete it.

Critical Inquiry Map ▶ ▶ ▶

In the center of the map, place the subject of an inquiry or the question you are investigating. As the map progresses, refer to Figure 3.3 to find the thinking skills categorized by stage in the Inquiry Process and list the appropriate critical thinking skills and their applications you might use at each stage. For example, if you are investigating gender differences in science learning, you might write, "Explaining why I think it is important to study gender differences in science learning" in the map area for Stage 1.

Critical Inquiry Map

Inquiry Topic: <u>Investigating gender differences in the acquisition of science-related knowledge</u>

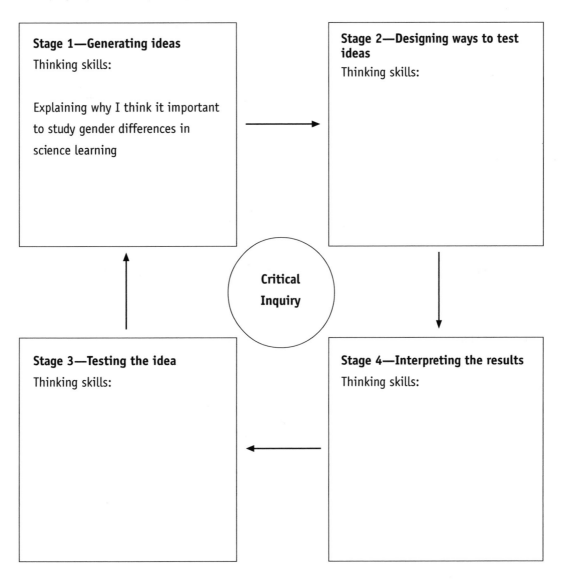

Stage 1—Generating ideas
Thinking skills:

Explaining why I think it important to study gender differences in science learning

Stage 2—Designing ways to test ideas
Thinking skills:

Critical Inquiry

Stage 3—Testing the idea
Thinking skills:

Stage 4—Interpreting the results
Thinking skills:

Card Storming ▷ ▷ ▶

Thinking together creatively is another way to use human resources to facilitate the development of a learning community. Card Storming supplies a strategy with which teachers can use to build consensus. In addition, Card Storming provides an alternative to traditional brainstorming activities.

1. Divide the group into subgroups of three to five participants seating so that everyone can see, hear, and speak together.

2. Distribute plenty of index cards to each group.

3. Elect a facilitator/speaker for each group.

4. Begin discussing the topic in small groups. Everyone in the group writes down different ideas on a separate index card.

5. Individual group members each order the ideas given from most important to least important.

6. Discuss the ordering of cards as a group and negotiate your group's order until consensus is reached.

7. Using a long strip of masking tape, order one set of cards that represents the group's consensus.

8. Attach each group's taped cards to a wall and begin the process again with the large group coming to consensus about one set of cards, listing ideas from most important to least important.

This card storming technique allows ideas to be ordered and reordered easily in any type of planning or problem-solving session. The cards also allow a clear view of the relationships among the ideas on the cards, a dimension not always possible when dealing with lists on easel paper or ideas written on boards.

COLLABORATIVE LEARNING AND LEADING

Over sixty years ago, Vygotsky (1978) introduced the concept of socio-cultural learning; that is, cognitive development and understanding are influenced by the social, historical, cultural, and political context of the learner. For example, when faced with a new concept or problem, teachers often seek advice from other teachers, administrators, or educational experts. They do so because educators want to know what other educators think and what they have experienced. Moreover, the classroom or school has its own context that is best understood by those who share it. The social nature of learning also means that it should involve talk and collegial relationships among different types of educators in a school or district so that multiple perspectives are available.

> Good Company and good discourse are the very sinews of virtue.
>
> — IZAAK WALTON

One new model for schoolwide or district-wide exploration and learning that uses the strengths of sociocultural learning is the collaborative learning group. A collaborative learning group often replaces staff development models that are dependent on outside "experts." These expert training models do offer information and instruction, but they also leave a participant with only the knowledge he or she has been able to glean as an individual and without a true understanding of how this knowledge can be applied. In contrast, collaborative learning groups concentrate on the needs or issues within a whole school so that professional development efforts explore common themes or questions on common ground. These groups also provide a forum for sharing different ideas and perspectives by persons actively engaged in finding solutions. Like all high-quality professional development, collaborative learning groups go beyond an individual learning activity to a learning process that pervades the group members' professional lives.

The formation of collaborative learning groups can be initiated by teacher-leaders or by an administrator. The size of the group should be limited to six so that all participants have the ability to speak and a common meeting time is possible. Membership in the group, however, should be voluntary.

The purpose of a study group is collaboration and learning—both professional activities that are violated by mandating participation. Once the group has been formed, the following functioning steps help secure proactive results:

1. Investigate the sociocultural variables—the social, historical, cultural, and political context of the situation.
2. Review rules for constructive criticism.
3. Engage in critical inquiry.
4. Assume responsibility for one's own learning.
5. Practice problem solving that focuses on results.
6. Plan for the implementation of decisions.
7. Implement decisions on a pilot basis.
8. Evaluate the results.

One illustration of the collaborative learning process is a program of study groups formed by the Lawrence Public Schools in Lawrence, Kansas. These groups, facilitated by a district instructional coordinator and comprised of six teachers and the principal, address a topic or problem. Functioning strategies within the Lawrence groups involve release time for regular meetings as well as peer coaching for support of classroom change. In describing the district's professional development support systems, Crowther, Division Director of Evaluations and Standards of Lawrence Public Schools reports, "Of all our initiatives, school-level study groups have had the greatest impact on changes in teacher behavior. Neither teachers nor principals want these considered during budget cuts" (1998, 76).

The circle of participants in a collaborative learning group will all be exercising leadership because an individual is transformed by a group, just as a group is transformed by its individual members. All stakeholders in the group have something to offer one another as they work in a common learning and problem-solving effort. In *The Practice of Teaching,* Jackson (1986) describes a type of educational practice that goes beyond changes in knowledge or technique as *transformative education.* Like transformational leadership, transformative education differs from traditional education in that it touches the inner core of an individual, affecting values and attitudes. When engaging in this transformative education, teachers would encourage discussion, demonstration, and argumentation, looking for "fuller participants in an evolving moral order" (Jackson 1986, 127). Collaborative learning groups seek this same type of education or learning. They are not, therefore, for the faint of heart or those who only wish to validate the status quo by going through the motions of review. However, collaborative learning groups that are formed correctly and function well can be very effective in connecting teacher-leaders. Utilizing the combined potential of its members, collaborative learning groups can engage in proactive, critical inquiry to bring about school transformation (see Figure 3.4).

STRATEGIES FOR COLLABORATIVE LEARNING AND LEADING

As collaborative learning groups begin their work, the emphasis first must be on collaboration. Collaboration does not mean automatic or enforced consensus or "groupthink." Welch and Sheridan define collaboration as "a dynamic framework for efforts which endorses interdependence and parity during interactive exchange of resources between at least two partners who work together in a decision-making process that is influenced by cultural and systemic factors to achieve common goals" (1995, 11). While this view of collaboration sustains the sociocultural aspect of collaborative learning groups, it also introduces the notion of resources that go beyond opinions or ideas of people. Like any organization, schools have many

Collaborative Learning Groups—Forming and Functioning

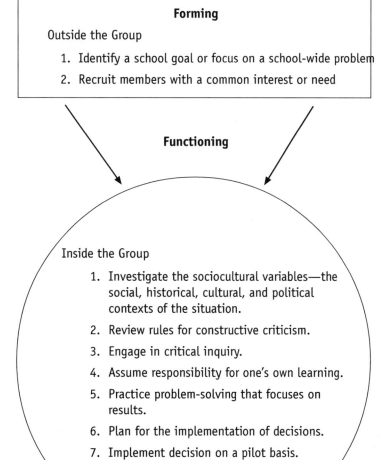

Forming

Outside the Group

    1. Identify a school goal or focus on a school-wide problem

    2. Recruit members with a common interest or need

Functioning

Inside the Group

    1. Investigate the sociocultural variables—the social, historical, cultural, and political contexts of the situation.

    2. Review rules for constructive criticism.

    3. Engage in critical inquiry.

    4. Assume responsibility for one's own learning.

    5. Practice problem-solving that focuses on results.

    6. Plan for the implementation of decisions.

    7. Implement decision on a pilot basis.

    8. Evaluate the results.

Figure 3.4

layers of resources, which by their abundance or scarcity, impact every type of transformational effort. Maher and Bennett (1984) report five different types of resources within an organization: personnel, information, technology, physical facilities, and finance.

Ideally, a collaborative learning group would include among its members persons with knowledge of these different types of systemic resources so that all could be involved in the interactive exchange as the group makes decisions. For example, teachers with knowledge of content areas are important in setting benchmarks for school standards, but such teachers must also have input from others who know about the technology and physical facilities required, have information about the state requirements, and be aware of the financial support available. Even collaborative learning groups for novice teachers should include representation from experienced teachers so that discussions are not limited to one level of knowledge or experience.

Collaborative learning groups, then, focus on a schoolwide problem to study, learn, and seek a solution. But they also build community and challenge the thinking of their members. Birchak et al. clarify these additional benefits experienced by collaborative learning groups with whom they worked: "We gradually came to understand that the two purposes were not in opposition to each other but were both essential to the study group process" (1998, 16). The sense of trust that really knowing other group members advances can actually make discussion and thinking critically about one's own practices easier.

Call to Collaborative Inquiry, Learning, and Action ▶ ▶ ▶

The following offers an organizing template for a Collaborative Learning Group as it is formed and begins to function.

1. Goal or Problem of the Group

2. Membership of the Group

3. Meeting Day and Meeting Length

4. Beginning Date of Group _____   Ending Date of Group_____

5. Questions to be Explored

6. Sociocultural Variables

7. Desired Outcomes

8. Resources Needed

9. Information Needed

10. Team Role for this Session

11. Action for Next Session

Collaborative Learning and Mentoring

One of the most valuable areas in leadership and collaboration is the movement toward mentoring. The word *mentor,* meaning a trusted counselor or guide, is taken from the name of a friend of Odysseus to whom he entrusted the education of his son, Telemachus. An education mentor, like Telemachus's teacher, does more than teach academic lessons or engage in clinical supervision; the mentor also provides collegial support. A teacher/mentor can be assigned as a resource to a new teacher entering a school system, as a partner to a more experienced teacher, or as a guide in a particular skill area such as technology.

When working with a new teacher, a mentor would see that her or his mentee was familiar with the facilities and routines of the school. These orientation activities, however, are surface courtesies and soon finished. A true mentor helps a new teacher structure lessons when needed, observes teaching and gives constructive feedback, and offers encouragement throughout the year.

With varying roles and time commitments, mentoring is an individualistic type of collaboration. Crow and Matthews see the persons involved in mentoring as travelers, guides, and passengers: "Travelers are those wanting and needing assistance. Guides are mentors for the travelers. Passengers are those on the journey who also benefit from the mentoring process" (1998, 3). Benefits for the travelers are many: "exposure to new ideas and creativity, visibility with key personnel, protection from damaging situations, opportunities for challenging and risk-taking activities, increased confidence and competence, and improved reflection" (Crow and Matthews 1998, 10-11). There are also benefits to the guides that strengthen leadership behaviors and build confidence. These benefits are grounded in reflection, the occasion to talk about teaching methods and ideas, personal satisfaction, and the possibility of learning from the traveler.

Traveling the mentoring road is not without its bumps, however. Heller and Sindelar (1991) reported that mentors need to be aware of three major challenges: they must avoid dependency from the mentee; they should be able to let go at the appropriate time, and they should not allow themselves to be drawn into an assessment role. On the other hand, mentees sometimes complain that a mentor's attention is short-lived, that mentoring sometimes may actually limit decision-making, and that mentoring activities fall off sharply as the year progresses.

Using the Finding the Middle Road strategy that follows, potential mentors/teachers can outline realistic expectations that would balance the benefits and concerns for both the mentor and the novice teacher.

Finding the Middle Road ▶ ▶ ▶

Describe your expectations for the roles of the guide and the traveler below.

As I guide I would:

As I guide, I would expect a traveler to:

How does the mentoring experience strengthen the leadership behaviors in the REACH model?

- Risk-taking:

- Effective:

- Autonomous:

- Collegial:

- Honorable:

Looking Back/REACHing Forward ▶ ▶ ▶

Professional Growth and Development

Chapter 3 began with the metaphor of school as a learning laboratory. Within that laboratory, the professional growth and development of the teacher-leader was the subject of study. Consider your current learning environment and professional development program as you complete the statements below.

My learning environment is like . . .

I never knew that . . .

Professionalism is a vital part of teacher-leadership because . . .

The possibility of a collaborative learning group sounds like . . .

Communicating Leadership

▶   ▶   ▶   ▶   ▶   ▶   ▶   ▶   ▶   ▶

Success in the art of teaching and leading cannot occur without communication competence—the ability to analyze, organize, and present concepts and ideas well. It is no accident that these are also the skills required in critical thinking, for one complements and advances the other. In order to have understanding, one must have language and the ability to use it well. Communication is not just speaking or writing words, it is the creation and naming of meaning.

The knowledge base that controls content in educational disciplines is often emphasized more than the presentation of that knowledge because content can be catalogued and classified, norm-referenced and ranked; knowledge of content is "provable." While communication skills are also rooted in content knowledge, the use of those skills involve presentation practices that are judged more subjectively and are presumed to evolve with teaching experience. Yet the practice of weak communication skills in the classroom or in the boardroom only evolves into bad habits and may, in fact, inhibit or negate communication attempts by affecting the perception of a teacher-leader's competence. Strong communication skills, on the other hand, evolve from understanding exactly what communication is and how it works. Teacher-leaders who exhibit positive communication skills are perceived as more effective: they are seen as more knowledgeable, competent, and empathetic because they speak, write, and listen well.

Research studying the correlation between effective leadership skills and effective communication has found that leaders seek new information, ask for feedback, and easily exercise their abilities to persuade others to consider their ideas (Bass 1990). Teacher-leaders' good communication habits and skills are simply a part of who they are and evidence of their leadership potential. As the REACH model expands in Figure 4.1, it reflects the developing capabilities of a teacher-leader. The placement of communication skills indicates communication skills may be renewed and enhanced through professional development as well as the integral part communication plays in successfully employing all the REACH teacher-leadership behaviors.

The REACH Model

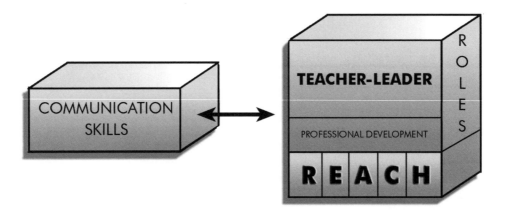

Figure 4.1

EFFECTIVE COMMUNICATION FOR TEACHER-LEADERSHIP

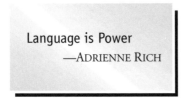

Language is Power
—ADRIENNE RICH

Communication involves the transfer of a message from sender to receiver. This communication triad (shown in Figure 4.2), depends on all three parts to complete one act of communication. The sender generates the meaning—encodes it into a message that is sent verbally or non-verbally. The acts of encoding and sending both require thinking on the part of the sender. The message, or intended meaning, consists of symbols called words or symbolic actions that nonverbally convey meaning.

Effective communication exists when the receiver interprets the sender's message in the same way the sender intended. However, "noise" (any distraction that interferes with sharing the message of the meaning) can break into the communication triad at any point. Any situation provides stimuli that may first induce or suppress the sender's ability to encode and send as

The Communication Triad

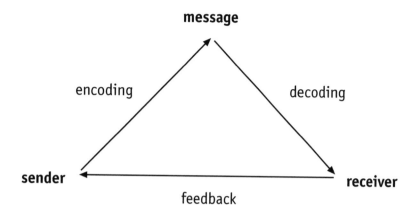

Figure 4.2

well as the receiver's ability to decode, receive, and/or give feedback. For example, a private message sent to a teacher by phone may be encoded and received correctly, but the teacher may not be able to give appropriate feedback because he or she is in a room full of students. The cycle of communication may then break down.

Teacher-leaders take the Communication Triad very seriously because they understand that language use is a human construction that reflects thinking and creates perceptions. Just as the arrangement of a classroom illustrates a pedagogical philosophy and approach, sound communication skills depict social sensibility, model intelligence, and represent an openness to others' messages. Slick communication skills may look impressive and effective, but if they do not encourage independent thought or are dishonorable in intent, they are counterfeit. Whether sharing knowledge with students, collaborating with colleagues, or interacting with administrators, teacher-leaders need to develop communication strategies that carry their messages convincingly and mark them as capable.

The communication skills necessary for formal presentations that teacher-leaders may give are the same skills used in informal presentations, group work, or communication with an individual student, parent, or colleague. Only the situation is different; the point or the end goal is the same—making connections. Educators who wish to share their ideas are sensitive to the complex variables that impact the total communication act and change strategies accordingly.

As a sender, it is the responsibility of a teacher-leader to see that the message is encoded as competently and sent as clearly as possible. This means that a sender must use audience analysis to know the characteristics of her or his audience and the possible impact of the message upon that audience. When using audience analysis, a sender considers three major areas of concern to the receiver:

1. **Psychology**—the sender heeds *selective perception*—the tendency of receivers to respond to a message not as it is, but as they are. Receivers are also generally *egocentric*—they listen and respond best to messages that are meaningful to them personally.

2. **Demographics**—the sender reflects about the impact of demographics upon receivers. The comfort level and vocabulary required in a message is related to the *age* of individual receivers and/or the composite age of a group of receivers. The use of inclusive language and careful analysis of the message avoids inadvertent *gender stereotypes*. Attention to *cultural background* also necessitates a careful use of vocabulary and inclusion of group interests and references. Even the *physical location* of the receivers can affect their capability to understand and empathize with a message.

3. **Situation**—the sender observes any situation that influences the receivers' acceptance of a message. The *size* of the group controls a sender's volume of voice and strength of gesture, the type of media he or she can use, and the relative formality of the delivery. The *receivers' disposition to a topic* indicates their collective interest in, knowledge about, and attitude toward a message. The *receivers' disposition to a speaker* pertains to the degree of approval the sender inspires through competence and credibility. On the other hand, the *receivers' disposition to the occasion* conforms to the understanding of an assignment, agreement with the taste or decorum of the sender, and acceptance of the time involved in the presentation.

The delivery of a message or presentation itself is not staged as a "performance," but always undertaken with the idea that the sender is communicating *with* a receiver or group of receivers, not *at* them. The effectiveness of oral delivery, developed through knowledge and practice, is limited only by the speaking ability and creativity of the sender. In order to perform most successfully, the sender needs to analyze his or her own speaking abilities in the following categories:

- Pitch—the highness or lowness of the voice.
- Rate—the pace at which one speaks
- Inflection—the change or lack of change in a person's voice
- Volume—the loudness or softness of the voice
- Enunciation—the pronunciation and articulation of the sounds of the words
- Paralanguage—the use of specific sounds and silences
- Nonverbal cues—the body language of the sender in general and gestures used specifically to stress or reinforce parts of the message

Communication without language is possible only on the most primitive level, because understanding is necessarily dependent on language use just as skill in language aids understanding. From this perspective, skillful communication is not only necessary for effectiveness in teaching, learning, and leadership; skillful communication is also a learning tool for heightening and refining thinking.

STRATEGIES FOR EFFECTIVE COMMUNICATION

Utilizing the Communication Triad of Sender-Message-Receiver as a guide will help teacher-leaders reach their audiences. The impact of the message upon those audiences is another consideration. The communication strategies in this section examine structuring the message itself so that it carries the intent of the speaker and maintains the interest of the receiver.

The message's organization makes the meaning clear and provides for its logical progression. In discovering knowledge, the speaker may organize the information through a variety of designs, including those below:

> A word is dead
> When it is said,
> Some say it just
> Begins to live
> —EMILY DICKINSON

- Classification—a sorting by definition and category
- Operation—a sorting by stage-phase, cause-effect, need-plan, or beginning-end
- Structure—a sorting by whole-part or the physical relationships.

After the sender chooses a method of organization, he or she also needs to compose an opening statement so that all of the main points of the presentation lead to the residual message—that which is remembered when the presentation is over. For example, although the particulars of Martin Luther King's *I Have a Dream* speech may be fuzzy, most audiences who have heard it clearly remember his call for racial equality as well as educational, social, and economic equity.

The opening statement of any presentation sets the tone of the communication and appeals to the audience's interest. Such a statement may be a quotation, statistics, a profile, a question, a startling statement, a story, a demonstration, or humorous anecdote. For example, the opening statement of the education report *A Nation at Risk* used war rhetoric to startle the reader and emphasize the seriousness of the message. "If an unfriendly foreign power had attempted to impose on America the mediocre educational performance that exists today, we might well have viewed it as an act of war" (National Commission on Excellence in Education 1983, 1). Whatever the device chosen, the opening statement strives to catch attention and/or creatively introduce the subject.

The arrangement and style of a presentation allows it to flow instead of sputter and falter. Language, the medium of the message, is shaped by environment, general culture, education, training, beliefs, attitudes, even moods. Naturally, presenters should model grammatically correct, unbiased, and nonsexist language use, but their language should also be creative, compelling, and even fun. Creative "markers" that make presentations exciting and memorable follow in the following strategy, Creative Markers and Their Effects. Teacher-leaders can use the examples on the left side of the page as models of language strategies to apply creative communication in their classroom, collegial, or formal presentations.

Creative Markers and Their Effects

Creative Markers for Presentations

1. Repetition

Repetition, repetition, repetition acts as a stimulus-response. The same signal reinforces the same response as in slogans and jingles. The effect of repetition is relatively short-lived and can be annoying if overused.

Example: *We shall pay any price, bear any burden, meet any hardship, support any friend, oppose any foe to assure the survival and success of liberty.* (John F. Kennedy)

2. Involvement

Involvement acts as personal response that usually involves a call to action. As the demand of the personal involvement increases, the skill of the presenter must also increase.

Example: *Uncle Sam needs YOU.*

3. Fear

Fear acts on the need of people to feel safe. This strategy can backfire if the fear induced causes the receiver to tune out the rest of the message or to feel hostile toward the person creating the atmosphere of fear. When used effectively, fear can raise the consciousness of a receiver.

Example: *Problem—nuclear weapons. At ground level a nuclear bomb would convert all people and property in a 3/4 mile radius to radioactive particles. Six miles from the site, all would be killed. Twenty miles from the site, all would be killed. Property damage would be complete.*
Solution—eliminate the threat of nuclear war by eliminating nuclear weapons.

4. Joy

Joy acts as happiness discovered or remembered. Joy creates warm fuzzies for the receiver to feel good about.

Example: *Our school ranks first in the nation in ACT scores!*

5. Emulation

Emulation acts as a call to follow a leader who is respected. The leader chosen for emulation should fit the audience and purpose of the presentation.

Examples: *Peace Corp volunteer, Mother Teresa, Michael Jordan*

6. Humor

Humor acts as a device to provide enjoyment or entertainment through the clever use of language or situations.

Example: *Restaurant prices at the nation's House of Representatives Dining Room are twenty-five percent higher than last year. This proves that the House is truly like a home.*

7. Metaphor

Metaphor acts as a device to relate the unfamiliar with the familiar. An extended metaphor can act as an advanced organizer with parallel points of structure presented in figurative language and can act as the controlling image in a presentation.

Examples: *In a Station of the Metro*
The apparition of these faces in the crowd;
Petals on a wet, black bough. (Ezra Pound)

COMMUNICATION WITH STUDENTS

Only those having torches will pass them on to others

—PLATO

Classroom communication presents a classroom teaching and learning paradox that teachers face daily. They are exhorted to construct meaning with each student and meet her or his individual needs while managing groups of students at the same time. The multiple and sometimes overlapping verbal and nonverbal communication cues that a teacher-leader uses to organize an experience and support students' learning constitute one of the distinctions between a novice and an expert teacher. Handling multiple and overlapping verbal and nonverbal cues is not easy, but like all communication skills, this can be learned and always improved. Strong classroom communication is interwoven in all aspects of REACH teacher-leaders' behaviors and is vital to establishing a secure, active, and productive environment.

In a study of five diverse teacher-leaders, LeBlanc and Shelton (1997) found that all of the teachers listed good communication skills (listening, self-confidence, humor, truthfulness, and reliability) as the most important skills needed in teacher-leadership. One teacher stated, "You have to know how to interact with people. You have to be believable...People have to feel that—how do I want to put it—you're discussing something with them because you really value their opinion" (LeBlanc and Shelton 1997, 40). Since the landmark study of *Pygmalion in the Classroom* by Rosenthal and Jacobson (1968), teachers have known that they can influence students' achievement by communicating to them verbally or non-verbally that there is a certain behavior expected of them. Positive expectations can raise the degree of effort, while negative expectations encourage a student to descend into learned helplessness. Moreover, the implications of brain-based learning and constructivist pedagogy encourage teachers to look at relationships as they reflect about the communication patterns found in their classrooms. For example, Wubbels and Levy (1993) stress that all aspects of a communication system are interrelated and circular—they consist of behaviors that, in turn, determine other behaviors. Teacher behavior affects teacher-student interactions that affect student behavior. Student behavior then affects teacher behavior and the cycle begins again. Despite interruptions, people who are communicating continually exchange messages that reply to earlier messages.

To be successful in the classroom, teachers need to understand the relationships embedded in communication just as students need to know the communication rules—when, where, and how to communicate. Communication rules that call for different activities or behaviors are termed participation structures because they determine appropriate ways to participate (when to raise one's hand, for example). Students' perceptions of these participation structures may be confused and become a source of misunderstanding with the teacher. This type of dysfunction can be exacerbated by a variety of perceptions due to cultural, socioeconomic status, age, and even gender differences.

If the same language used by teachers and students in a classroom does not ensure communication, what can? Woolfolk suggests that teachers "make communication rules for activities clear and explicit" (1995, 187). The examples below help clarify participation structures for both teachers and students:

- Do not assume students know what you want them to do.
- Signal students when their participation is required.
- Teach and model appropriate behavior and positive communication.
- Expect all students to participate at their highest level.
- Use consistent participation structures.
- Reward positive communication and use of classroom participation structures.
- Practice active listening.

A person practicing active listening pays close attention to what is said, considers the message and the point of view, and shapes appropriate responses. Listening is complicated: it involves the filtering of many stimuli (the noise in communication) before some are selected. Yet O'Keefe maintains that "improving our relations with others really begins with listening" (1995, 91). This improvement in relationships is possible because active listening indicates an interest in understanding another's perspective by considering it carefully. A teacher-leader can signal active listening to her or his students in the following ways:

- Face the speaker and use alert body language as you listen.
- Assume natural eye contact and an interested facial expression.
- Focus on the message being sent rather than your reaction to the message.
- Try to hear the feelings of the person speaking.
- Clarify what you hear by restating it or asking questions if the message is unclear.
- Allow students to speak for a reasonable amount of time without interrupting.
- Respect a student's right to speak or question as long as the language is appropriate.
- Ask questions to allow a student to shift perspective.
- Help students understand that no one need listen to hateful speech.

Obviously, active listening behaviors should be grounded in sincerity, or they will communicate a message of hypocrisy and deceit. In classrooms marked by effective communication, teachers commonly go beyond facts and rote information to construct meaning and question general assumptions. As leaders concerned with maintaining and improving relationships with their students, they must use communication skills to go beyond language to the real message of learning and learners.

STRATEGIES FOR COMMUNICATING WITH STUDENTS

> We teachers can only help the work going on, as servants wait upon a master.
>
> —MARIA MONTESSORI

In seeking to build a new image of schools and a new conception of the voice of teachers in that image, Schlechty (1990) examines the notion of a "knowledge worker." The time of public education preparing the blue-collar worker for a career in industry has passed. The Industrial Age has been realized. This is now the Information Age where the most precious commodity is knowledge. Students do come with some knowledge, but one assumes that their knowledge will be increased as a result of being in knowledge-work organizations called schools.

If a student is recognized as an active participant in working to gain knowledge, she or he is also a responsible member of a classroom learning community, not a blank slate waiting to be written upon by a teacher. In this type of classroom learning community, the teacher's role shifts from the expert to the facilitator, requiring "the teacher to shift from the role of information processor and inspector to the role of manager and leader" (Schlechty 1990, 240). As a teacher shifts from repeating information to interchanging ideas and constructing meaning, the importance of effective communication is apparent.

The knowledge-work communication shared by teachers and students operates best when it not only delivers a message accurately between sender and receiver, but also supports and strengthens the relationship between them. Figure 4.3 "Building Relationships through Classroom Communication" lists the characteristics that support and build relationships.

A teacher's voice and communicative manner can nurture or repress student learning. It is a power that demands no less than the highest sensitivity and the finest communication skills a teacher-leader can develop.

Building Relationships through Classroom Communication

▶ Address problems constructively by directly addressing the problem, not personalities.

▶ Stay in touch and understand your own feelings and how they influence behavior.

▶ Keep nonverbal communication congruent with verbal communication; that is, make sure that a student is receiving the same message verbally and nonverbally. For example, positive reinforcement should be accompanied by a warm, direct nonverbal presence so that both types of feedback are consistent with one another.

▶ Accept responsibility for your own attitude and behavior.

▶ Validate students' contributions even if their ideas are later discarded.

▶ Treat all students with consistent respect and acceptance.

▶ Listen well and actively.

Figure 4.3

Applying Classroom Communication That Builds Relationships ▶ ▶ ▶

Applying the concepts outlined in Figure 4.3, "Building Relationships through Classroom Communication" requires awareness both of how that communication would sound (the verbal message) and how it would look (the non-verbal message). Imagine a teacher-leader facing a student who has been repeatedly disruptive today. The teacher has given the student a fifteen-minute detention after school and now has the opportunity to build a relationship with this student while discussing the problem. Describe the communication that would be most effective in building relationships using the chart below. For example, a teacher-leader addressing the first concept would begin by verbally focusing on the problem, not the student by asking, "How do consistent interruptions of classroom discussion limit the benefit of those discussions for students?" This verbal question would be accompanied by an interested and open nonverbal facial expression, signifying a willingness to listen to what the student has to say.

Classroom Communication That Builds Relationships	Verbal Communication	Nonverbal Communication
1. Problem-oriented, not personality-oriented.		
2. Understand teacher's own feelings and influence of behavior.		
3. Keep nonverbal and verbal communication congruent; that is, make sure that a student is receiving the same message verbally and non-verbally.		
4. Accept responsibility for your own attitudes and behavior.		
5. Validate students' contributions.		
6. Treat all students with respect and acceptance.		
7. Listen well.		

COMMUNICATION WITH FAMILIES

What families have in common the world around is that they are the place where people learn who they are and how to be that way.

—JEAN ILLSLEY CLARKE

Families are the first teachers and the longest teachers. However, modern families defy simple classification or a single approach. Modern families are complex; half of all marriages now end in divorce. Foster families and extended families raise a greater percentage of children every year. Modern families are diverse; single parenthood is common, second marriage families are common, blended families are common, and families with gay and lesbian parents are becoming more common. Modern families are busy and stressed for time; over seventy-six percent of mothers work outside the home.

Despite these divergent family combinations, social classes, and financial opportunities, however, modern families generally share some common attributes: they care deeply for their children, and they want their children to do well in school. Yet in 1999, the National Center for Educational Statistics reported that forty-seven percent of teachers surveyed indicated that they disagreed or strongly disagreed with the statement that they received a great deal of support from parents (p. 41).

Communicating with families is not always easy, but that communication is absolutely necessary for building a relationship of trust and cooperation between the adults who have the greatest influence over students' success. Often communication between teachers and families is marred when teachers think families of troubled students are headed by deficient parents. If one is deficient as a parent, the false perception contends, then he or she cannot be a useful partner in their child's learning. Lack of family involvement in school activities is often misread as an indication of such a parental deficit. Negative assumptions about families can make both sending and receiving messages difficult. The opposite, though none the less challenging, situation teachers face is when families are intrusive and difficult, when they seem too deeply involved in classroom processes. Froyen suggests "a teacher who gives them the benefit of the doubt can generally convert good intentions into appropriate interventions" (1993, 318–319).

Moving beyond these communication inhibitors and reaching families also requires understanding social factors that may keep families from having strong school relationships. A student's parents or caregiver may be reluctant to be involved with or communicate with teachers if there is conflict or abuse in the home. They may be embarrassed about a lack of control or feel that their parenting skills are inadequate. Parents or caregivers who have a personal history of failure in school are also reluctant to communicate. In this situation, the teacher is the personification of the system that failed them or they failed. In either case, the communication is uncomfortable. A language barrier is another factor that can produce a real division between school and home, while parent work hours and teacher work hours may cause connection problems. Add to this growing list families' lack of transportation, lack of understanding of current teaching/learning practices, and reluctance to take on any more responsibility, and the extent of the problem becomes more apparent. Understanding these factors, however, may also suggest alternatives, ways of communicating that reassure, indicate empathy, and show respect.

With communication initiated, what type of family involvement is appropriate and meaningful? Teacher-leaders will find few parents that really don't care about their children. What families do need, however, are clear suggestions about how they can help by becoming partners with teachers in their children's education. Sometimes this means that a family member will need to speak up for a child or explain circumstances at home which may be affecting the student's achievement at school. Other times, a teacher-leader will need to initiate contact or ask for help with a student. This type of open communication requires building more than communication skills; it also involves using those communication skills either individually or in groups to increase trust between home and school.

Communication with families about the opportunities for active involvement in their student's education can occur through the familiar parent-teacher conference. This idea may be expanded and enriched by having a three-way conference in which the student develops speaking skills and confidence by explaining his or her portfolio materials and progress to the family. This conference option should be supported by child-care available at the school to assure that the child who is speaking has the undivided attention of the adults present. Other communication opportunities include the following:

- Open houses in which the teacher invites the parents to speak or take home a survey about their child's interests, strengths, and needs
- Quarterly or monthly newsletters in which the teacher or students outline the activities of the class and report good news
- Formal reporting of assessments and student progress and permission forms for special activities
- Parental contributions to the academics of the school through classroom presentations about careers, cultures, experiences, or specialized knowledge.

Less formal occasions for communication with families arise through phone calls, notes sent home, and extracurricular functions. Many schools are now equipping their classrooms with phones and answering machines. This allows the teacher to leave the day's objectives and assignments on an answering machine message that both students and parents can access for clarification. Such a phone messaging system also allows a parent to leave a message for the teacher or to request a telephone call at a specific time of day if the teacher is not in class. E-mail, the forming of listserv groups, or Internet sites for classroom sharing are other electronic formats for communication. These computer-based systems are exciting, but they can be both time-consuming for the teacher-leader and frustrating to the family if they are not current. Enlisting the help of students to keep Internet sites up-to-date can help, but this type of student assistance must also be monitored so that any communication presented is appropriate and contains the correct information.

Communication may also be facilitated in additional creative ways. For example, family members speaking to the class or even taping interviews or stories to be shared with the class communicates both the content of the presentation/story as well as the value of learning. Family members might also lend support by locating resource materials, conversing with students about their experiences at school, serving as chaperons or field trip escorts, or arranging special teaching/learning experiences.

Whatever the occasion, communicating in an open, honest manner will make further communication more comfortable. In a series of teacher reflections, Tertell et al. (1998) present a teacher's voice who shares how she maintains good relationships with the families of her students. "In my interactions, I always tried to convey three ideas: the value of the child, the family's important role in the child's life, and my commitment to both the child and the family" (Tertell et al. 1998, 153).

While communication with families can be difficult and time-consuming work, the development of reciprocal relationships with families represents leadership that can truly optimize the learning experiences of students and exemplify the REACH model in action.

STRATEGY FOR COMMUNICATING WITH FAMILIES

> What is or was is not necessarily what ought to be.
>
> —B. EDWARD MCCLELLAN

As families and teacher-leaders work together to help students learn, they need to be aware of one another's expectations and their own attitudes toward those expectations. If either of the parties thinks that the other is unreasonable, then communication will most likely falter. Froyen (1993) asserts that since a teacher most often initiates a school-family relationship, she or he must be also nurture it and be aware of the following expectations parents generally have of teachers:

- Be concerned about their child; be interested in the characteristics that define the child as a unique person.
- Teach their child; help their child acquire the foundations for lifelong learning, learn how to interact successfully with others, and understand and appreciate the achievements of humankind.
- Inspire their child to want to learn and to make the most of the opportunities the school has to offer.
- Stimulate their child's efforts to celebrate attainments and cultivate aspirations.
- Help their child develop self-control.
- Keep them apprised of their child's progress and of any difficulties that might require their cooperation.

- Work diligently and earnestly to make the most of the community's investment in education and to address parents' concerns for their child's well-being.

Adapted from *Classroom Management: The Reflective Teacher-Leader,* 2nd edition by L. A. Froyen. © 1993 by Macmillan, Inc., New York. Reprinted with permission.

In the following Family-School Expectations Projection activity, Froyen's research-based list of parental expectations of teachers has been placed in one half of a Venn diagram. The other half of the diagram is left open for teacher expectations of themselves as classroom teacher-leaders. Where would these expectations overlap? Where would they disagree? What expectations might teacher-leaders have of themselves that are not included in the list? Information about expectations specific to a community or type of school could be gathered at Open Houses and added to Froyen's list to inform later discussions.

Family-School Expectations Projection Strategy

In the Teacher Expectation area that follows, teachers can fill out the expectations they have for themselves in this school year. Family expectations listed above have been entered in the Family Expectation area. Which areas overlap or project common ground? Which areas project a significant difference in perception or expectation? Discuss your Expectations Projection with another teacher and a family member of a student. How does understanding one's own and other's expectations influence communication and behavior?

Family Expectations
1. Be concerned about their child and interested in the child as a unique person . . .
2. Teach their child, help their child . . .
3. Inspire their child to want to learn . . .
4. Stimulate their child's efforts to celebrate attainments . . .
5. Help their child develop self-control.
6. Keep them apprised of their child's progress . . .
7. Work diligently and earnestly and address parents' concerns . . .

Common Ground

Teacher Expectations

COMMUNICATION WITH COLLEAGUES

The notion of communicating with colleagues assumes connections among individuals that go beyond a nod and "mornin'," to sharing ideas and finding collective wisdom and strength. Boyer (1995) reports that when surveyed in 1994, only five percent of teachers supported working alone. Teachers generally prefer working together to plan and implement curriculum, undertake professional development, and complete school projects.

Forming and maintaining groups of teachers to work together does not happen easily just because it is preferred. Working groups of teachers need time, a supportive organization, and trusting, positive relationships among themselves to function well. The element of time is straightforward—teachers need time to meet, to think, to plan, and to collaborate. However, to function well as a group, teachers also need a school culture that encourages them to risk collaboration and rewards them for developing the positive relationships that empower groups.

The culture of a school refers to its dominant patterns, its visions and missions, and the experiences of the common community. Whatever its nature, it is deeply felt as a positive or negative factor in teacher satisfaction and performance. However, Hopkins et al. argue that school improvement strategies that consider and address internal conditions can lead cultural change, and "it is the cultural change that supports the teaching-learning process which leads to enhanced outcomes for students" (1994, 196). Furthermore, Kurpius (1991) asserts that the culture of an organization is the most powerful factor in determining the degree of collaboration among its members. While teacher-leaders are dependent on a supportive school culture for success, they also help create that culture through collaboration. In this way, collegiality creates the environment in which leadership for all teachers may thrive.

Why seek collaboration? Don't teachers have enough to do? Certainly building positive interpersonal relationships with others takes energy and interpersonal communication skills, but the rewards justify the efforts and enhance REACH behaviors in the following ways:

- Collaboration can create professional, personal, and moral support as teachers engage in **risking** new things.
- Collaboration can encourage shared learning and improved teaching as teacher-leaders explore new ideas and empower one another's efforts, thereby becoming more **effective** and time-efficient.
- Collaboration can actually increase a teacher-leader's confidence in her or his **autonomous** initiatives and decisions by providing a support group to inform those initiatives and decisions.
- Collaboration allows new types of relationships and communication among teachers-leaders and administrators, counselors, and other stakeholders, reflecting **collegiality**.

> It is still true no matter how old you are—when you go into the world, it is best to hold hands and stick together.
> —ROBERT FULGHUM

SkyLight Professional Development

- Collaboration provides the strength of numbers for supporting behaviors that model **honor** and the integrity to speak up for what is right when the politics of a situation might encourage silence and conformity.

Unfortunately, the road to collaborative relationships is not always a smooth one. There are barriers to collaboration that, as hindering forces, must be considered and removed. Welch (1998) summarizes these barriers into four categories: conceptual barriers, pragmatic barriers, attitudinal barriers, and professional barriers. Conceptual barriers occur when the conception of roles and traditions within a school culture have become rigid and reinforced by notions of "the way things are," or "the way things are done around here." Pragmatic barriers, on the other hand, occur when systemic and logistic factors interfere. Bureaucratic organization and lack of time are two very common pragmatic barriers to collaboration. Because organizations are composed of humans, emotions and attitudes can create barriers. Sometimes these attitudes are based in fear and uncertainty; other times they can end in disappointment and disillusionment following unrealistic attitudes about how easy collaboration will be. Finally, the education profession itself can be a barrier to collaboration when colleagues lack background in conflict resolution, effective communication, or a philosophical commitment to its importance. Yet Darling-Hammond and Sclan emphasize that "virtually all of the most recent research on school leadership connects teacher commitment with a more collaborative and value-based style of leadership—one aimed at enhancing professional commitment, using symbolic and transformational values as touchstones" (1996, 86).

STRATEGIES FOR COMMUNICATING WITH COLLEAGUES

When educators engage in team-building exercises, they are really building interpersonal relationships and exploring collaborative communication skills. As team members seek to achieve effective collaborative communication, they need to give and take. They need to give their ideas and best efforts to the group while taking seriously the adoption and use of Steps to Collaborative Communication as illustrated in Figure 4.4.

Within Step 1 of Building Collaborative Communication, a group needs to spend some time developing consensus about the goal, objectives, processes, and individuals' roles for the group. Consensual decision making requires both opportunities to share and compromise: each member of a group has an equal opportunity to share his or her views and make contributions, and when, necessary, group members should compromise their views to have a working consensus within the group that is acceptable to all members. Crawford et al. explain that consensual decision-making is a strong strategy because a "unified commitment to implementation of the

Steps to Collaborative Communication

6. Reflecting about action and outcomes

5. Practicing critical inquiry

4. Employing collegial communication that reinforces the postive and deals honestly with conflict

3. Using listening behaviors that show respect and interest

2. Seeking and honoring contributions by all members

1. Clarifying for understanding the goal/purpose of the collaborative group

Mature Collaborative Communication

Early stages of Collaborative Communication

Collaborative Communication Processes

Figure 4.4

decision may be expected since implementation follows agreement reached before the decision was made" (1997, 137). For example, a minority of members who have been outvoted in a democratic decision could block implementation of a decision by refusing to participate. With consensual decision making, however, the group has agreed at the outset to come to consensus and hence to implement a compromise that is acceptable to the group. Obviously, every decision a group makes may not be consensual, but the goals, objectives, processes, and individuals' roles within a group should have consensual parameters.

The keys to developing collaborative communication through Steps 2, 3, and 4 are respect and acceptance. This is not an acceptance that is synonymous with polite tolerance, but a commitment to sharing personal experiences, ideas, and alternatives with an open mind. When conflict occurs, group members deal with it openly and honestly. Birchak et al. explain that conflict can be healthy and actually plays a significant role in personal and professional growth, recognizing if there is unanimous agreement, there is nothing to discuss: "It's through conflict and difference that we are challenged to define our theory and articulate what we believe" (1998, 118).

The mature stages of collaborative communication are inclusive of earlier stages, but add the inquiry and reflective characteristics of problem-solving that are necessary to finish the work of the group. Reflection is also appropriate, however, for group members to consider the influence of membership upon their own practice and the impact of the group's work on the culture of the school. Individual reflection after collaborative experiences is important because communication processes may follow general rules, but they still require individual decisions and strategies.

Moving from the early stages to the mature stages of collaborative communication requires knowledge and experience. It also involves a conscious choice to remain strong and focused with courtesy and restraint—to persist, but in a collegial manner. The "Strategic Planning Session" case study that follows poses a problem not just for the individuals involved in the discussion, but the entire group.

Strategic Planning Session

Even though the temperature was cool, the atmosphere inside the library conference room was heated. Members of the task force for strategic planning shifted uneasily in their seats as Jonathon, one of the most outspoken members, insisted that the multicultural curriculum under discussion would simply divide the student population into ethnic cliques. "If they are citizens, they are Americans," he declared. "We should be about finishing the melting pot that our ancestors started and building one culture, not multiple ones. It will only confuse the students." Jonathon was answered by Kate who offered that the melting pot theory never did work; that's why it was left unfinished. "Nonsense!" Jonathon exclaimed. "I don't think of myself as German; I think of myself as an American. This is the way it should be. This is the attitude we all need to have if we are going to be one country!"

Fran, the elected teacher-leader of the task force, mentally reminded herself of the stages of collaborative communication as she glanced around at the group members who had turned to her. What she said next would have to address the conflict itself, but how she said it would set the tone for the rest of the meeting.

How might Fran lead the group from Step 1 to Step 5 of collaborative communication?

Looking Back/REACHing Forward ▶ ▶ ▶

Excellent communication skills begin with understanding that communication is the creation and naming of meaning and knowing how to encode and decode that meaning effectively. Teacher-leaders use communication skills to teach and to learn as well as to interact with their students, students' families, and colleagues at all levels within the school. Use the space below to reflect about how communication within each of these areas has changed in the last decade and how it has remained the same.

Communicating Leadership

Areas of Communication for Teacher-Leaders	Communication Strategies That Have Changed in the Last Decade	Communication Strategies That Have Remained the Same in the Last Decade
Classroom Communication While Teaching and Learning		
Communicating with Students as Individuals		
Communicating with Students' Families		
Communicating with Colleagues		

CHAPTER 5

Connecting Teacher-Leaders

▶   ▶   ▶   ▶   ▶   ▶   ▶   ▶   ▶   ▶

T he exercise of teacher-leadership develops naturally as one's learning communities evolve. Communicating change and sharing ideas outside the classroom or school certainly requires a vision, but practically it also requires a platform or situation and appropriate leadership strategies to be successful. This chapter will discuss two different situations in which teacher-leaders might interact and network with other professionals outside their own school buildings to exchange educational ideas:

- Professional Organizations and Publications
- Teacher Exhibits and Educational Conferences

The key to a professional exchange among teacher-leaders is sharing ideas that challenge and affirm critical thinking and inquiry, resulting in the establishment of human networks that not only seek answers, but ask hard questions and invite one to act at a higher level. Entering into these types of networks is a type of constructivist activity: knowledge is actively constructed in terms of prior learning, attitude, personal experiences, and social/cultural environments. Human networks also offer experientially rich learning contexts as well as opportunities for decision-making and collaboration that encourage learning, promote collegiality and an identity with a group of professionals, strengthen teaching, and nurture leadership skills. In fact, McLaughlin (1995) reports higher achievement among students of teachers who were involved in learning communities because teachers who learn together influence one another and are more likely to sustain positive change. Strategies that empower human networks connect theory with practice, teacher-leaders with other teacher-leaders, and individuals with their own potential in a two-way interaction illustrated in Figure 5.1. The teacher-leader reaches out to professional organizations and publications for new knowledge and extends his or her teaching and learning through teacher exhibits and educational conferences. The outcomes of these outreach activities are learning and opportunities for exercising leadership—strategies for strengthening REACH behaviors.

The REACH Model

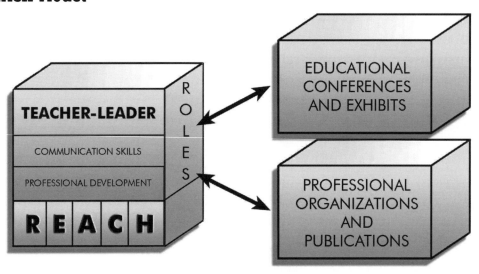

Figure 5.1

PROFESSIONAL ORGANIZATIONS AND PUBLICATIONS

> We teach what we learn, and the cycle goes on.
> —JOAN L. CURCIO

Professional organizations in education have increasingly seen themselves as learning communities, disseminating information and sponsoring preparation, renewal, and enhancement activities for their members. Indeed, Gene Glass, President of AERA (American Educational Research Association) affirms that AERA is dedicated to the concept of a professional learning community when he asserts, "It exists to communicate knowledge and ideas…" (1998, 35). Active membership contributes to the professional development of teacher-leaders when they take advantage of the educational opportunities and collegial connections offered through professional organizations. Consider the chance of a teacher finding someone in the same hall of her or his school who shares the same interests, experiences the same problems. The probability would be rather small. Now consider that same teacher finding someone in a state or national organization with the same interests and problems. The probability would be increased significantly.

As teachers move through their careers, they often encounter different cycles of professional development. Fessler and Christensen (1992) report a framework that includes eight levels: preservice, induction, competency building, enthusiastic and growing, career frustration, stable and stagnant career, wind-down, and career exit. The first four levels are a building time when teachers eagerly attend professional organization conferences and meetings, read publications, and often share their ideas and experiences/ research. The new information and research about teaching and leading supplied by professional organizations are important support systems for teacher-leaders in these stages of their careers. The last four levels, however, often involve dissatisfaction and/or disappointment with career potential and experiences. For teachers in these stages, professional organizations are especially significant in helping them revitalize efforts and understand how valuable they can be as mentors and leaders in their schools.

Professional membership may also supply criteria for professional advancement when members obtain specialized certification through them. For example, The National Board for Professional Teaching Standards offers advanced certification for teachers nationwide who meet its standards, just as the National Strength and Conditioning Association offers a CECS certificate (Certified Strength and Condition Specialist) for professionals in health education.

Many professional organizations also offer publication opportunities for all educators or related experts. For teacher-leaders with unique ideas or research to share, a professional periodical or journal offers the opportunity to reach a wide audience while the idea or research is fresh. Both professional journals and periodicals are published regularly, but they differ in what they publish. Scholarly journals generally contain formal research while periodicals may include some research but also accept thought pieces, historical reviews, editorials, or field reports.

STRATEGIES FOR INVOLVEMENT WITH PROFESSIONAL ORGANIZATIONS AND PUBLICATIONS

Professional organizations offer different types of support for educators as outlined as follows:

- Subject Specific—focusing on a particular subject matter or a particular type of students (e.g., National Science Institute)
- Pedagogical—focusing on new methods, curricular design and innovation, school reform, and the advancement of teaching/learning (e.g., Association for Supervision and Curriculum Development, National Education Association, American Federation of Teachers)

- Specialized Functions—focusing on research, assessment, or other specific issues (American Educational Research Association).

Although membership is usually just a matter of paying dues, the involvement with these organizations varies with the opportunities they offer and the needs of an individual. Membership in teacher unions (NEA, AFT) also offers professional connections, but this membership is obtained through employment with public school districts that affiliate with one or the other. Originally formed to engage in collective bargaining for teachers, these unions are now also concerned with professional development and educational reform at the local, state, and national levels. National and state organizations generally have Internet sites that simplify learning about them and getting involved. The easiest way to find these sites is typing their names into a search engine and then going to the homepage ending in ".org" that will be listed among the search results. Limiting an electronic search to the organization's initials (such as AEA) can lead to frustration and enormous lists of sites that contain those letters in their homepage titles.

Electronic communication within professional organizations provides specialized networks and connections for their members through E-mail, listservs, chat rooms, and forums. Subject-specific organizations also serve their members electronically and often supplement communication with lesson plans, photographs, sound bytes, and other resource materials. In addition, many professional organizations are now offering listings of jobs and hints about finding a position in education.

Seeking certification from professional organizations certainly marks leadership among teachers who are willing to demonstrate their proficiencies. The goal of the National Board for Professional Teaching Standards, for example, establishes "high and rigorous standards for what teachers should know and be able to do and to certify teachers who meet those standards" (1989, iii). Teachers who wish to be certified by this organization must videotape and analyze their lessons, write reflectively, prepare a professional portfolio, and take written exams. Is all this work worth it?

The authentic nature of the assessment activities for National Board Certification verifies the connections between teachers, students and teachers, and subject content and pedagogy. Darling-Hammond explains, "The participatory nature of the accompanying assessment systems supports wide development of knowledge throughout the profession, enhancing the establishment of shared norms by making teaching public and collegial" (1999, 39). While this type of public documentation risks public failure, the rewards benefit all the human networks that include a certified teacher.

Professional Publications

Before submitting any article to a professional publication, there are a number of considerations that increase the likelihood of acceptance and publication:

1. Match the topic, the audience you are trying to reach, and your personal goals with a journal or periodical.
2. Research the acceptance rate and response time of the publications you are considering.
3. Include some research data to support your position or theory. However, consider the audience when reporting research and avoid a mini-thesis approach.
4. Investigate the theme issues that publications are planning to see if your manuscript falls within a theme.
5. Polish your writing by making the text neat, free of misspelling and grammatical errors.
6. Conform to the length specified by the publisher.
7. Follow stylistic requirements particular to a publication.

A potential author generally can find style and format information as well as the address for submission and the editor's name from the front, inside panel of a professional publication. Moreover, looking at circulation numbers can provide data about how many possible readers a publication has. However, actually reading several issues of the targeted journal best lends insight into what type of writing style and subject matter the editors prefer.

When the manuscript is polished, printed, and presented, authors settle into a period of waiting, not unlike expectant parents, while the work is reviewed. Positive reviews are gratifying, just as negative ones are unsettling, but they both produce learning and reflection. Reviews and rejections should be used to clarify and adapt the material, not as reasons to discard it. Checking the acceptance rate of journals can also be discouraging for an unpublished author. But rejection, although painful, is not fatal. It is often a step in the writing-rewriting cycle that leads to a stronger work and the satisfaction of seeing one's ideas in print.

TEACHER EXHIBITS AND EDUCATIONAL CONFERENCES

The locations in which teachers traditionally share their ideas—the school parking lot or the teachers' lounge—are less than ideal for interaction and reflection. Consequently, teachers' searches for the live presentation of new knowledge and ideas lead them to exhibits by other teachers and professional development sessions at educational conferences. An exhibition or conference provides a situation in which teaching, learning, and sharing

> Make no little plans; they have no magic to stir [people's] blood and probably themselves will not be realized.
>
> —DANIEL H. BURNHAM

about a variety of topics can take place quickly. Moreover, exhibitions and conferences are seen as opportunities for showcasing the work of a particular learning community. This learning community could be a group of teachers going through a Master's degree course on teacher-leadership or a group of teachers undertaking professional development through their schools. In both scenarios, exhibits and conferences can be seen as a way to display and celebrate professional growth. They serve as both closure to a learning project and as something to share with colleagues, school leaders, and parents as well as the community at large.

The *Oxford Encyclopedic English Dictionary* defines exhibit as "a product to show or reveal publicly for interest, amusement, in competition, etc; submit for consideration." Although all teacher exhibits do offer the opportunity to show what is known, the format of exhibits may be of three types:

- Individual exhibits such as teaching portfolios
- Exhibits of discovery within a specific subject or topic by a learning community
- Thematic exhibits which provide educational information by a number of different individuals, but related by theme

While teacher-leaders may be most familiar with the format and value of teaching portfolios, this type of exhibit does not often serve to establish outreach and human networks. The evolving practice of teacher exhibits of discovery and thematic exhibits, however, provide exciting possibilities for the creation of empowering contexts for sharing. An exhibit of discovery takes the critical inquiry of a learning community to the next level, applying the classroom experiences of the group to discovered knowledge and sharing the result as part of professional development or school reform. The discovery of a learning community may be shared through a report, an electronic presentation by representatives of the group, a panel presentation by the entire group, or a case study of the issue—all collaborative products that can be utilized by other educators. An example of this type of teacher exhibition would be a report that proposes an innovative approach to at-risk programming researched and compiled by a district-level learning community.

A thematic exhibit, on the other hand, is also a group event, but it is focused about a topic of broad interest with individual exhibits that address the theme or investigate different parts of a districtwide issue or problem. This type of exhibit reflects how teacher-leaders perform in the classroom—they plan, prepare materials, teach, assess, and reflect so they may also learn. This type of exhibit also offers an educationally useful product or series of products related by theme, prepared by individuals or small groups. Examples of this type of exhibition would be poster sessions of a number of applied research projects, presentation of classroom-based field studies, teaching modules or activities to be shared, learning center kits, resource directories, a collections of writings, or even a video illustrating different applications of a teaching model. The thematic exhibition opens windows of commonality across grade levels and disciplines while extending leadership opportunities for participants in planning, organizing, and presenting.

On a larger scale, while it is not possible for an entire staff of a school district to attend an educational conference at a distance, it is possible that a conference can come to them. A district-wide or regional educational conference can involve teacher-leaders as planners, and include them as presenters in a district-wide professional development conference provided on site. Planning and executing a teacher-led conference is a significant exercise in REACH teacher-leadership behaviors, challenging teachers to be creative, organized, and professional, while encompassing all the strong design and positive communication skills that they can muster. This type of leadership can also encourage teachers attending to learn new strategies, share successful methodologies, and connect with others in the school district interested in the same issues.

Why would teacher leaders want to stage a conference or an exhibition of their teaching and learning? The main reason to hold an exhibition or conference is to disseminate educational information on a large scale in a central location within a limited amount of time. Other purposes—problem solving, motivation or inspiration, decision making, learning purposes—are also related to and dependent on communicating information and ideas.

Classroom teachers sharing information about their own action research findings or innovations in exhibitions or conferences provides recognition of their leadership activities and adds the voice of the teacher to the fund of knowledge about effective educational practice. The influence of the teacher's voice upon both educational theory and practice is supported by Cochran-Smith and Lytle as vital for the entire profession: "We need to develop a different theory of knowledge for teaching, a different epistemology that regards inquiry by teachers themselves as a distinctive and important way of knowing about teaching" (1993, 43). Other benefits include the enhancement of organization and communication skills that provide confidence in the exercise of teacher-leadership, the opportunity to practice self-reflection and obtain feedback, and activities that support school goals. Both teacher-leader exhibitions and educational conferences promote renewal and a new spirit of inquiry that advances professionalism and leadership through reflection, performance, research, and a collegial sharing of expertise.

STRATEGIES FOR DISCOVERY AND THEMATIC TEACHER EXHIBITIONS

Teacher exhibitions are authentic approaches to presenting shared understandings and assessing the outcomes of learning communities. A relatively new trend in education, exhibitions create opportunities to give and gain information as well as to evaluate professional growth in a positive manner. Evaluation often suggests accountability that, in turn, implies minimal standards of performance. But assessment should also be a vehicle for identifying excellence. Learning to teach and learning to lead are both developmental processes that should extend over the professional life of a teacher. Likewise the assessment of these processes should reflect the measures by which a teacher grows and develops. Engaging in an exhibition gives the participants ownership in their own professional development and control about how they will show growth.

How does one go about staging an exhibition? Obviously, the organization of the exhibition depends upon the number of participants and its purpose. Strategies for forming Collaborative Learning Groups (see chapter 3) will get the group moving in a proactive manner. The purpose of the exhibition will govern arrangements for facilities and resources. Will this be a panel presentation to the school board or a full day of professional development mounted district-wide? What useful educational products will result from the exhibit? Despite the wide range of possibilities, all teacher exhibitions share an emphasis on reflection as teacher-leaders consider what to present and how to present it. Accordingly, teacher exhibits should include evidence of the following elements in Figure 5.20.

Elements of a Teacher Exhibit

- Mastery of a specialized skill or expertise in a subject or issue
- Impact on student performance
- Decision-making shaped by analysis, evaluation, and execution of possible change
- An explicit application professional values—the articulative, operational, and political dimensions of teaching
- A pilot plan for transformation
- An effective use of presentation materials and resources

Figure 5.2

Whatever the final product of a teacher exhibition, the process of staging the exhibit gives teachers roles, responsibilities, and rewards that are real. This strategy for teaching and learning offers an alternative to the sideways motion of many teachers' careers by helping them build upward, practicing leadership and establishing their own authentic identities.

Elements of a Teacher Exhibition on Teacher-Leadership ▶ ▶ ▶

As stated earlier, one of the major benefits of teacher exhibitions is reflection by teacher-leaders as they decided what to present and how to present it. Using the elements of a teacher exhibition as a guide, a teacher-leader can reflect about her or his growth and development in teacher-leadership during the past year and indicate what type of evidence he or she would provide within each element for a thematic exhibition on teacher-leadership.

Evidence of outcome provided:

Mastery of a specialized skill or expertise in a subject or issue:

Impact on student performance

An explicit application professional values—the articulative, operational, and political dimensions of teaching:

A pilot plan for transformation:

An effective use of presentation materials and resources:

How does the evidence given above relate to the REACH model of teacher-leadership?

STRATEGIES FOR PLANNING AND STAGING AN EDUCATIONAL CONFERENCE

A conference is a meeting of at least two or more persons who come together to exchange information or discuss issues of common concern. As the number of persons involved in a conference increases, the complexity of the arrangements and planning also increases. The mark of effective planning, however, is evident when the conference participants are not aware of the planning process, but are able to enjoy what seems to be a project that flows well and has it own energy. To achieve this state, planners must become designers who go beyond planning the conference to producing it, focusing on one goal—a smooth dissemination of information.

Organizing Decisions

As conference planners meet for the first time, they are faced with three major decisions that should be made before any designing is done:

- What is the purpose of the event? (**WHAT?**)
- Who is expected to attend the event? (**WHO?**)
- How will the planning and execution of the conference be accomplished? (**WHEN, WHERE, HOW?**)

These questions are not listed in order of importance, but are interrelated and mutually dependent. While they will need to be discussed separately, they should each be considered as individual units before conference planners make final decisions about the execution of the conference.

The purpose of an academic conference is its *goal* that then drives its outcomes. Conference planners must select activities that will work for the event, their projected audience, and their resources. Behind the generally abstract question of the goal are questions that describe outcomes:

- Will the conference sustain the philosophy of the host institution?
- Will the conference offer a unique perspective or information that can be considered substantive?
- Will the conference generate interest? The established goal of an academic conference becomes its theme and influences its name.

The organizing decisions about the purpose of the conference also include a determination of the scope of the event:

- Will it have local, district, state, or national appeal?
- Will it encompass specific training or include several strands of related presentations?
- Will it contain workshops offered by experts in a specific area?

Closely related to the decision about purpose is the consideration of participation:

- Who will come?
- What will they expect?
- What level of knowledge about the issues can be assumed?

The activity decisions (When, Where, How) may likewise influence the purpose and participation decisions. "When" and "Where" are control factors for matching dates, sites, resources, and needs. "How" is at the heart of design, moving beyond the abstract to action. Usually, the action stage begins when the conference planners (the Committee of the Whole) elect a conference coordinator and divide the labor into committees with clearly specified tasks. Outlining tasks carefully may take patience and time, but it saves frustration and conflict that might arise when certain committees' tasks overlap or a chain of communication is not understood.

Organizing People and Tasks

The coordination of a conference is a time-consuming, but rewarding task for a person comfortable with situational leadership. It is not possible to attend to all the details of a large conference personally, so the coordinator will oversee a number of committees that function independently of one another, but in cooperation with all. The coordinator is the center or core of communication, ensuring that each committee is aware of the progress of the others. He or she must be a person with strong organizational skills, a feel for the audience, and awareness of connections or willingness to form connections to obtain resources—a teacher-leader who exemplifies the REACH model.

The election of a conference coordinator and determination of a theme are usually completed before the "committee of the whole" breaks into specific committees with specialized tasks. Because the theme of the conference is a type of template for all the committees, general endorsement of the theme is a necessary step (see Worksheet A1 in the Appendix for a sample Initial Planning Sheet). Each member of the committee of the whole is assigned an important part in designing and executing the master plan. This establishes what needs to be done by whom. Committee functions then determine the details of "how" the conference will operate.

Committee Functions

Initial planning makes an event happen. Individual committees then assume the task of turning the event scheduled to happen into a "happening." No one special committee is more important than the others—all committees are needed to reach the common goal—but the sequence of work may be different depending on the tasks performed.

> A committee is a group of people that keeps the minutes and loses hours.
> —MILTON BERLE

The Design Committee

The design committee develops ideas for the theme of the conference, establishes the general outline of presentations, invites or selects presenters, then coordinates decorations and overall conference program design to reinforce the theme with style. Style is hard to define; it means different things to different people. Generally, however, it reflects polish and sophistication, but still manages to generate excitement and fun.

The theme of a conference is visually communicated by a graphic depicting the theme, the "logo" of the conference. The importance of this logo is echoed by its appearance on all communications about the conference, the program, the signs, and the invitations. If the conference presentations are not set, the design committee follows one of two methods to complete the selection: a refereed or invitational process. A refereed selection process involves advertising for presentation proposals and evaluating those subsequent proposals by a jury of experts. An invitational process, on the other hand, does not require advertisement or evaluation. Presenters are invited to speak based on their expertise and experience until all the time slots of the conference are filled.

The conference program, produced by this committee, presents the theme of the conference, lists all participants, and clearly identifies the place, time, and topic of the presentation. Room chairpersons may or may not be used to introduce speakers and keep strict account of the time allotted each speaker in the sessions, but even if chairpersons are not used, the schedule must be maintained. Related to the design committee's task of conference program construction is the careful inclusion of all sponsors and special awards or acknowledgments. This program is the first inclusion in the conference packet that is distributed to all conference participants, but it should also be posted and available at other points for quick reference.

The heavy work of the design committee occurs at the beginning and toward the end of the planning process. The day of the conference, the design committee decorates the banquet rooms and takes responsibility for posting a program and other important information. Because other committees are dependent on the results of the design work, the design committee needs to function responsibly and with a great deal of creativity. Worksheet A2 in the Appendix provides a committee plan sheet for all committees to register tasks, while Worksheet A4 in the Appendix can help appropriate deadlines for internal committee use.

The Development Committee

Once a date, time, site, and theme have been chosen, the development committee moves forward to make concrete arrangements—to develop the design through the following tasks:

- Examining the facility and making a detailed floor plan available to the media committee

- Assigning rooms for all the sessions
- Determining the menu for any meals
- Making arrangements for seating and serving at those meals
- Assuming the responsibility for directional signs
- Preparing rooms and signs the day of the conference

A visit to the facility soon after the committee has been formed is a must. Traffic control decisions hinge upon the number of entrances, the proximity of the rooms to one another, accessibility, number of elevators, width of stairs and hallways, places to deposit coats, as well as other possible uses of the facility the same day. The location of lounge areas and refreshment areas, and the existence or nonexistence of smoking areas all make a difference when assigning rooms. In addition, many conference sites book more than one event for any given time, so directional signs must be clear.

The actual seating and equipment arrangements within a function room (the setup) depends on the needs of the presenter, the number of participants expected, the room size, and the resources available. Most facilities do their own setup early on the day of the conference, but the development committee is responsible for checking that setup matches the diagram of the room that the committee has used to plan. Other considerations germane to room assignment are fixed platforms, acoustics in the room, the location of electrical outlets, availability of sound systems, carpeting, types of chairs, natural light and/or controlled lighting, controlled heating/cooling, fixed screens or boards, light fixtures, mirrors, pictures, even the location of phones.

Early decisions by the development committee about menus are also imperative because the cost of the conference is directly related to food and facility costs. Food and beverages should complement the event, not overshadow it. The banquet room, too, needs a setup plan. Round tables seating ten that invite conversation are typically used in a large hall. When using round tables that seat eight to ten persons, the following equation will provide a guide for number of guests, allowing comfortable spacing between tables.

Length of Hall x Width of Hall ÷ 10 = Maximum Number of Persons

The development committee's work is not done when arrangements are finished. This committee also makes or sees that directional signs are available and in place the day of the conference and that the rooms are ready. Using the graphic logo of the conference helps identify the signs if more than one event is scheduled at a site, and color always enhances the visual effect. Satisfactory seating arrangements are confirmed at least one hour before the start of the conference so that replacements can be provided before the participants enter the room. Water for the presenter(s) is provided fifteen minutes before the conference begins and refreshed as needed.

SkyLight Professional Development

Technology Committee

Lights, cameras, action! The visual and audiovisual part of conference presentations cannot take place without the accurate investigation and painstaking checking of the technology committee. This group also needs to visit the site of the conference or carefully consult floor plans for the location of electrical outlets and the availability of equipment at the site. If there is a display room, the technology committee will need to contact presenters and find out what type of equipment the presenters anticipate needing both in a function room and in the display hall.

The function room where break-out sessions occur may have limitations that have to be modified when utilizing technology (only one or two outlets, for example, or unblocked natural light that might interfere with electronic projection). The members of the technology committee do not have to be technical experts, but they should review the basic setup of all equipment used. Because they are ultimately responsible for checking the equipment out or renting it from an outside source, this committee will not only set up the equipment, they will take it down following the sessions (unless the presenters are responsible for bringing their own). A two-day conference may require storage at the site and setup the second day if the function rooms cannot be secured. Other essential efforts when using media include the following actions:

- Tape down all electrical wires that cross traffic aisles with safety tape or duct tape so that they are not inadvertently disconnected or trip someone.
- Use surge protectors to create a number of outlets for equipment.
- Locate emergency numbers of technicians that can be called upon to help in an emergency (preferably at the site).
- Check ALL connections to make sure they are tight and test ALL equipment before the conference begins.
- Check the position of a viewing screen to make sure it can be seen from all vantage points.
- Provide backup supplies of extension cords, surge protectors, safety tape, lightbulbs for projectors, an extra VCR to circulate, adapters for PC and Macintosh computers, magic markers, blank transparencies and pens, and masking tape.
- Bring some basic tools (screwdrivers, needlenose pliers, scissors, etc.) for setup and simple repair.
- Notify security and traffic control at a site about the conference so that parking, delivery, and pickup of equipment can be handled smoothly.

A technology checksheet should be provided for each presenter. (An example of a technology checksheet can be found on Worksheet A4 in the Appendix.) Completed check sheets are then tallied to identify all technology equipment needed and where it should be placed.

Publicity Committee

Imagine giving a party that no one attends. It is the primary job of the publicity committee to see that this does not happen, to see that the conference, which other committees have designed and planned so carefully, is well attended. To that end, the publicity committee collects information about the presenters for local, district, and state release through various media. As the public relations connection for the conference, this committee also acts as hosts for the convention itself, attending to the personal needs of the presenters (supplying them with nametags, programs, packets, etc.) and making sure that the participants are comfortable and enjoying themselves.

The publicity committee's first function is a general announcement of the event. This announcement presents a broad overview of the conference and may be distributed two or three months previous to the event so that interested persons will be able to reserve the date. Besides clearly stating the theme, title, place, date, time, and cost, the initial announcement may also describe the benefits of attending the conference. Why should the potential audience members wish to come? Using the graphic logo of the conference at this time establishes a visual link later when the formal invitation arrives.

Following a general announcement, the focus of the publicity committee becomes one of public relations. "Public relations goes far beyond mere publicity; it is concerned with transmitting the image of . . . everyone involved with producing the conference" (Nadler and Nadler 1987, 270). The image of the conference is released to the public through newspaper contacts, television and radio contacts, and through professional networks. Educators, for example, would want to tap into their own networks of area educators, State Department of Education officials and their publication, as well as school districts close to the site. School districts sending presenters and local newspapers in the presenter's areas are also contacts for which a news release has interest.

An effective news release should be limited to one page of clearly organized information. The name, place, date, and time of the conference should be prominent. Finally, the news release provides information about who may be contacted for further information. This name(s) and phone number(s) generally belong to the chairperson of the event or one of the publicity committee. Interviews about the conference are also handled by the coordinator of the conference or by publicity committee members. Worksheet A5 in the Appendix provides news release information for committee use.

The Internet is another important news release source. On-line organizations, listservs, and chat rooms will often carry announcements of a conference of interest to their members. The publicity committee in cooperation with the processing committee might also mount its own Web site with conference information and even on-line registration.

One week before the conference, the publicity committee prepares nametags for the presenters and helps the processing committee compile packets. The day of the conference, the publicity committee members become ambassadors of goodwill—greeting, directing, and making everyone feel welcome.

Processing Committee

Like the word "processing" which means "gradual changes that lead toward a particular result" (Merriam-Webster 1983, 917), the processing committee is one of operations that influence the tone of the conference. This committee's first tasks are to design the invitation for the conference, collect individual guest lists, and compile a complete list for mailing.

The invitation follows the general announcement with specific information about the site, date, time, benefits, etc., but adds the ingredients of cost and registration. This is also the time to send a map to the site and parking instructions to potential participants. The tone of the invitation is one of excitement, but the impression should again be one of professionalism. The formal invitation also contains a registration form with a complete mail-back address and mail-back instructions for efficiently gathering registrations. Some invitations may be hand-delivered as a mark of respect or special interest, but all invitations should be received at least one month preceding the event with a preregistration due date two weeks to ten days preceding the conference. All committees will have to be updated about the registration numbers as they start to arrive.

The initial guest list is accumulated from all the conference planners and presenters, through organizational membership, and interest groups. Creating a computer database and mailing list from these guest lists are not only helpful for this particular conference, but for conferences that will follow. If an electronic database of people who have attended the conference in the past exists, it should still be checked against guest lists for current names and addresses.

If the mailing is to be metered, a careful sorting by zip code speeds up the delivery process. Contacts with the local post office are vital, so that the mailing conforms to all regulations. At this point, the success of the conference rests with the processing committee and their dependability. Mailing deadlines must be met.

After the invitations have been mailed, the committee then turns to preparing for the big day. Although other committees provide the contents of the registration packet, the processing committee obtains the folders and nametags from the host site, receives other materials, and assembles the registration packets at least one week prior to the conference. The processing committee also prepares or collects the evaluation forms for the conference and places a general evaluation form in each folder. Worksheet A6 in the Appendix provides such a form. Finally, signs for the registration table and registration instructions, prepared well in advance, complete the pre-conference working of the processing committee.

The day of the conference, the processing committee conducts the registration with skill and a smile. A welcoming table with coffee and juice also helps move traffic from one point to the next, just as a clearly marked point for the deposit of evaluation forms smooths the exit. All of these preparations are designed to start the conference promptly and positively.

The registration table(s) continue to function even after the conference has begun for late arrivals, to answer questions, to handle messages that may need to be conveyed, and to arrange for the collection of any evaluation that is to take place. Arrangements for staffing may involve some split times to keep the table covered for at least the first half day and during breaks. Whatever the format, the form is always one of graciousness and welcome, so that those who arrive as participants will leave as friends.

The business of the convention is finished, but the work of the convention goes on after the official event is only history. Careful planning and leadership leads this situation to a valued learning/sharing experience. The participants' "after-conference" work is to transfer and share what seems useful to their schools and classrooms, continuing to lead as professionals and teachers.

Taking the Big Step ▷ ▶ ▶

In the space below, a teacher-leader can provide answers to the three major decisions about an educational conference. These answers could then be used as a base for a proposal to a school district to provide professional development on-site. A proposal of this nature need not be extensive, but would include the basic organizational factors and the benefits to be derived from exercising teacher-leadership.

What is the purpose of the event? (WHAT)?

Who is expected to attend the event? (WHO?)

How will the planning and execution of the conference be accomplished? (WHEN? WHERE? HOW?)

How will this conference benefit the school district?

Looking Back/REACHing Forward ▷ ▶ ▶

All strategies that connect and strengthen teacher-leaders' REACH behaviors strengthen the teaching profession, because individuals *do* transform the larger group. The need for human networks engaged in transformation is real and immediate as the evolution of education continues. Teachers, who see themselves as professionals, know that they must claim their heritage with pride, their teaching and continued learning with responsibility, and their future with hope and the confidence of leaders. In this last reflection, comment on your ideas for change and progress in an evolved educational system.

Appendix

The following forms have been compiled to aid in the organization and implementation of strategies for staging an educational conference.

CONFERENCE INITIAL PLANNING SHEET

Name or Theme of Conference: _____

Supporting Details: _____

Conference Chairperson(s): _____

Telephone: (Day) _____ (Evening) _____

Date of event: _____

Time: _____

Committee Assignment: _____

Responsibilities:

_____

_____

_____

_____

_____

_____

_____

_____

Committee Chairperson(s): _____

Telephone: (Day) _____ (Evening) _____

Meeting Dates:

COMMITTEE PLAN WORKSHEET

Committee Name: _____
_____

Committee Responsibilities: _____
_____

Committee Chairperson(s): _____
_____

Members: _____
_____

Goal	Task	Who is Responsible?	Deadline Date

Worksheet A2 Committee Plan Worksheet

SkyLight Professional Development

COMMITTEE PLANNING SCHEDULE

Event: Date of Event:

Assignment	Person Responsible	Date to be Completed	Comments

Worksheet A3   Committee Planning Schedule

TECHNOLOGY EQUIPMENT REQUEST

Visual Equipment (Please indicate specific minimum needs):

PC Computer: Cite specifications needed (RAM, CD, disc, zip drive, Internet) _____

_____

Macintosh Computer: Cite specifications needed (RAM, CD, disc, zip drive, Internet) _____

_____

LCD panel(type, hookup) _____

Projector (type, hookup) _____

Slide Projector (sync, remote) _____

VCR/TV (large screen, portables, remote) _____

Overhead Projector(high-intensity, regular) _____

Screen _____

Easel/Flip Charts _____

Display Tables (Number, Size) _____

Audio Equipment:
❏ Tape Recorder
❏ Audio Cassette Player, Patch Cords
❏ Microphones (fixed, lapel, cordless)
❏ Piano
❏ Stands, Mike Stands
❏ Arrangements for Musical Entertainment

Miscellaneous:
❏ Cords
❏ Outlets, Strips
❏ Patch Cords
❏ Carts, Stands
❏ Podium
❏ Light for Podium

Technicians:
❏ Lighting and Sound System
❏ Computer Technicians

NEWS RELEASE INFORMATION

*To be completed by each presenter

Return to _____

Due Date _____

Name of Presenter _____

Topic of Presentation _____

Conference Name and Theme _____

Date of Presentation _____

Time of Presentation _____

For Further Information Contact _____

Business/Institution/School District Complete Address:

Local Newspaper Complete Address:

Worksheet A5   News Release Information

CONFERENCE EVALUATION FORM

Conference Name_____

Conference Site _____   Conference Date _____

Thank you for attending the _____Conference. We are interested in your responses to the events you have attended and invite you to fill out this evaluation to aid in future planning.

Please circle a number that reflects your opinion of the following statements:

	Disagree				**Agree**
1. The conference was well-planned Comments:	1	2	3	4	5
2. The presentations were effective. Comments:	1	2	3	4	5
3. The displays were valuable and informative. Comments:	1	2	3	4	5
4. Room arrangements were appropriate. Comments:	1	2	3	4	5
5. Use of technology was effective. Comments:	1	2	3	4	5
6. Parking was convenient. Comments:	1	2	3	4	5
7. The registration process was efficient. Comments:	1	2	3	4	5
8. Overall, the conference was valuable Comments:	1	2	3	4	5

Other Remarks:
What do you feel was the strength of the conference?

Anything you would like to suggest for future conferences?

Worksheet A6   Conference Evaluation Form

SkyLight Professional Development

References

Anderson, J. 1994. *Who's in charge? Teachers' views on control over school policy and classroom practices.* Washington, DC: Office of Educational Research and Improvement.

Barone, T., Berliner, D. C., Blanchard, J., Casanova, U., and McCowan, T. 1996. A future for teacher education: Developing a strong sense of professionalism. In J. Sikula, T. J., Buttery, and E. Guyton, (eds.) *Handbook of research on teacher education*, 2d ed. (pp. 1108–1145). New York: Macmillan.

Bass, B. M. 1990. *Bass and Stogdill's handbook of leadership: Theory, research, and managerial applications,* 3d ed. New York: The Free Press.

Bennis, W., and Nanus, B. 1985. *Leaders.* New York: Harper and Row.

Birchak, B., Connor, C., Crawford, K. M., Kahn, L. H., Kaser, S., Turner, S., and Short, K. G. 1998. *Teacher study groups: Building community through dialogue and reflection.* Urbana, IL: National Council of Teachers of English.

Bolman, L. G., and Deal, T. E. 1994. *Becoming a teacher leader: From isolation to collaboration.* Thousand Oaks, CA: Corwin Press.

Boyer, E. L. 1995. *The basic school: A community for learning.* San Francisco: Jossey-Bass.

Caine, R. N., and Caine, G. 1997. *Education on the edge of possibility.* Alexandria, VA: Association for Supervision and Curriculum Development.

Callahan, J. F., Clark, L. H., and Kellough, R. D. 1998. *Teaching in the middle and secondary schools*, 6th ed. Upper Saddle River, NJ: Prentice Hall.

Carnegie Forum on Education and the Economy. 1986. *A nation prepared: Teachers for the 21st century.* New York: Carnegie Corporation.

Clark, C. M. 1992. Teachers as designers in self-directed professional development. In A. Hargreaves and M. G. Fullan (eds.), *Understanding teacher development.* New York: Teachers College Press.

Cochran-Smith, M., and Lytle, S. 1993. *Inside/outside: Teacher research and knowledge.* New York: Teachers College Press.

Connelly, F. M., and Clandinin, D. J. 1988. *Teachers as curriculum planners: Narratives of experience.* New York: Teachers College Press.

Costa, A. L. 1991. *The school as a home for the mind.* Palatine, IL: Skylight Publishing.

Crawford, M., Kydd, L., and Riches, C. (eds.). 1997. *Leadership and teams in educational management.* Philadelphia, PA: Open University Press.

Crow, G. M. and Matthews, L. J. 1998. *Finding one's way: How mentoring can lead to dynamic leadership.* Thousand Oaks, CA: Corwin Press.

Crowther, S. 1998. Secrets of staff development support. *Educational Leadership, 55*(5), 75–76.

Danielson, C. 1996. *Enhancing professional practice: A framework for teaching.* Alexandria, VA: Association for Supervision and Curriculum Development.

Darling-Hammond, L. 1999. *Reshaping teaching policy, preparation, and practice: Influence of the National Board for Professional Teaching Standards.* Washington, D.C.: AACTE.

———. 1990. Teacher professionalism: Why and how? In A. Lieberman (ed.), *Schools as collaborative cultures* (pp. 25–50). New York: Falmer Press.

Darling-Hammond, L, and Sclan, E. M. 1996. Who teaches and why: Dilemmas of building a profession for twenty-first century schools. In J. Sikula, T. J. Buttery, and E. Guyton (eds.), *Handbook of research on teacher education* (2d. ed., pp. 67–101). New York: Macmillan.

Deal, T., and Peterson, K. 1990. *The principal's role in shaping school culture.* Washington, D. C.: U. S. Office of Educational Research and Improvement.

DeMarrais, K. B., and LeCompte, M. D. 1999. *The way schools work* (3d. ed.). New York: Addison Wesley Longman.

DuBrin, A. J. 1995. *Leadership: Research findings, practice, and skills.* Boston: Houghton Mifflin.

Fay, C. 1992. Empowerment through leadership: In the teachers' voice. In C. Livingston (ed.), *Teachers as leaders: Evolving roles* (pp. 57–90). Washington, DC: National Education Association of the United States.

Feimen-Nemser, S., and Floden, R. E. 1990. The cultures of teaching. In M. C. Wittrock (ed.), *Handbook of research on teaching,* (3d. ed., pp. 505–525). New York: MacMillan.

Fessler, R., and Christensen, J. 1992. *The teacher career cycle: Understanding and guiding the professional development of teachers.* Boston: Allyn & Bacon.

Forster, E. M. 1997. Teacher leadership: Professional right and responsibility. *Action in Teacher Education, 19*(3), 82–94.

Foster, K. 1990. Small steps on the way to teacher empowerment. *Educational Leadership,* 47(8), 38–40.

Froyen, L. A. 1993. Classroom management: The reflective teacher-leader (2d ed.). New York: Macmillan.

Fullan, M. 1993. Innovation, reform, and restructuring strategies. In G. Cawelti (ed.), *Challenges and achievements of American education* (pp. 116–133). Alexandria, VA: Association for Supervision and Curriculum Development.

Fullan, M. G. 1991. *The new meaning of educational change.* New York: Teachers College Press.

Glass, G. V. 1998. "The vision thing": Educational research and AERA in the 21st century—Part 4: The future of scholarly communications. *Educational Researcher,* 27(8), 35–37.

Griffin, G. A. 1990. Leadership for curriculum improvement: The school administrator's role. In A. Lieberman (ed.) *Schools as collaborative cultures: Creating the future now* (pp. 195–211). New York: Falmer Press.

Hall, G., and Hord, S. M. 1987. *Change in schools: Facilitating the process.* Albany, NY: State University of New York Press.

Hargreaves, A., and Fullan, M. 1998. *What's worth fighting for out there.* New York: Teachers College Press.

Heller, M.P. and Sindelar, W. 1991. Developing an effective teacher mentor program. Fastback 39. Bloomington, IN: *Phi Delta Kappan* Education Foundation.

Henson, K. T. 1990. Writing for educational journals. *Phi Delta Kappan,* 71(10), 800–802.

Hopkins, D., Ainscow, M, and West M. 1994. *School improvement in an era of change.* New York: Teachers College Press.

Jackson, P. W. 1986. *The practice of teaching.* New York: Holt, Rinehart, and Winston.

Jensen, E. 1995. *Super teaching.* San Diego, CA: The Brain Store.

Johnson, D., and Johnson, R. 1991. *Creative conflict.* Paper presented at Student At Risk Conference, October 1991, Drake University, Des Moines, IA.

Joyce, B., Weil, M., and Showers, B. 1992. *Models of teaching,* 4th ed. Boston: Allyn & Bacon.

Kurpuis, D. J. 1991. Why collaborative consultation fails: A matrix for consideration. *Journal of Education and Psychological Consultation,* 2, 193–195.

LeBlanc, P. E., and Shelton, M. M. 1997. Teacher leadership: The needs of teachers. *Action in Teacher Education,* 19(3), 32–45.

LeFrancois, G. R. 1990. *The lifespan.* Belmont: CA: Wadsworth.

Leithwood, K. A. 1992. The move toward transformational leadership. *Educational Leadership,* 49(5), 8–12.

Leithwood, K. A., and Jantzi, D. 1991. Transformational leadership: How principals can help reform school cultures. *School effectiveness and school improvement*, 1(3), 249–281.

Lewin, K. 1951. *Field theory in social psychology*. New York: Harper.

Lichtenstein, G., McLaughlin, M. W., and Knudsen, J. 1992. Teacher empowerment and professional knowledge. In A. Lieberman (ed.), *The changing contexts of teaching: Ninety-first yearbook of the national society for the study of education*. Chicago, IL: The University of Chicago Press.

Licklider, B. L. 1997. Breaking ranks: Changing the inservice institution. *NASSP Bulletin,* 81(585), 38–44.

Little, J. W. 1988. Assessing the prospects for teacher leadership. In A. Lieberman (ed.), *Building a professional culture in schools* (pp. 78I–106). New York: Teachers College Press.

Little, J. W. 1994. Teachers' professional development and education reform. In *Changing education: Resources for systemic reform* (pp. 154–160). Washington, DC.: U.S. Department of Education.

Maher, C. A., and Bennett, R. E. 1984. *Planning and evaluating special education services.* Englewood Cliffs, NJ: Prentice Hall.

McLaughlin, M. W. 1995, December. *Contexts for professional development.* Presentation delivered at the annual conference of the National Staff Development Council, Front Royal, VA.

Merriam-Webster New Collegiate Dictionary. 1983. Springfield, MA: G. and C. Merriam Co.

Mitchell, D. E., and Tucker, S. 1992. Leadership as a way of thinking. *Educational Leadership*, 49(5), 30–35.

Nadler, L., and Nadler, Z. 1987. *The comprehensive guide to successful conferences and meetings.* San Francisco: Jossey-Bass.

National Board for Professional Teaching Standards. 1989. *Toward high and rigorous standards for the teaching profession.* Detroit, MI: National Board for Professional Teaching Standards.

National Center for Education Statistics. 1999. *Teacher quality: A report on the preparation and qualifications of public school teachers.* Jessup, MD: U.S. Department of Education.

National Commission on Excellence in Education. 1983. *A Nation at risk: The imperative for educational reform.* Washington, DC: U. S. Government Printing Office.

National Education Association. 1975. *Code of Ethics of the Education Profession.* Washington, DC: NEA.

Oakes, J., and Lipton, M. 1999. *Teaching to change the world.* New York: McGraw-Hill.

O'Keefe, V. 1995. *Speaking to think, thinking to speak.* Portsmouth, NH: Boynton/Cook.

O'Loughlin, M. 1992. Empowering teachers in emancipatory knowledge construction, *Journal of Teacher Education*, 43(5), 336–346.

Pajak, E. 1993. Change and continuity in supervision and leadership. In
G. Cawelti (ed.), *Challenges and achievements of American education*
(pp. 158–186). Alexandria, VA: Association for Supervision and
Curriculum Development.

Popkewitz, T. S. 1994. Professionalization in teaching and teacher
education: Some notes on its history, ideology, and potential.
Teaching and Teacher Education, 10(1), 1–14.

Poplin, M. S. 1992. The leader's new role: Looking to the growth of
teachers. *Educational Leadership*, 49(5), 10–11.

Renyi, J. 1998. Building learning into the teaching job. *Educational
Leadership*, 55(5), 70–74.

Rosenthal, R. and Jacobson, L. 1968. *Pygmalion in the classroom:
Teacher expectations and pupils' intellectual development*. New York:
Holt.

Rowan, B. 1994. Comparing teachers' work with work in other occupations: Notes on the professional status of teaching. *Educational
Researcher*, 23(6), 4–17.

Schlechty, P. C. 1993. Schools for the twenty-first century: The conditions for invention. In. A. Lieberman (ed.), *Schools as collaborative
cultures: Creating the future now* (pp. 233–255). New York: Falmer
Press.

Schlechty, P. C. 1990. *Schools for the twenty-first century: Leadership
imperatives for educational reform*. San Francisco: Jossey-Bass.

Schmuck, R. A. 1997. *Practical action research for change*. Arlington
Heights, IL: Skylight Training and Publishing.

Scott, W. G., Mitchell, T. R., and Birnbarum, P. H. 1981. *Organization
theory: A structural and behavioral analysis,* 4th ed. Homewood, IL:
Richard D. Irwin.

Senge, P. M. 1990. The leader's new work: Building learning organizations. *Sloan Management Review*, 7–23.

Sergiovanni, T. J. 1990. Adding value to leadership gets extraordinary
results. *Educational Leadership*, 47(8), 27.

Sergiovanni, T. J. 1992. *Moral leadership: Getting to the heart of school
improvement*. San Francisco: Jossey-Bass.

Sirotnik, K., and Kimball, K. 1995. Preparing educators for leadership:
In praise of experience. Paper presented at the annual meeting of
the American Educational Research Association, San Francisco.

Sparks, D., and Loucks-Horsley, S. 1989. Five models of teacher development. *Journal of Staff Development*, 10(4), 40–57.

Sparks, D., and Hirsh, S. 1997. *A new vision for staff development*.
Alexandria, VA: Association for Supervision and Curriculum
Development.

Strike, K. A. 1996. The moral responsibilities of educators. In J. Sikula, T. J. Buttery, and E. Guyton (eds.), *Handbook of research on teacher education* (2nd ed., pp. 869–892). New York: Macmillan.

Talbert, J. E., and McLaughlin, M. W. 1994. Teacher professionalism in local school context. *American Journal of Education,* 102, 123–153.

Tertell, E. A., Klein, S. M., and Jewett, J. L. (eds.). 1998. *When teachers reflect: Journeys toward effective, inclusive practice.* Washington, DC: National Association for the Education of Young Children.

Truch, S. 1980. *Teacher burnout and what to do about it.* Novato, CA: Academic Therapy Publications.

Vygotsky, L. 1978. *Mind in society.* Cambridge, Mass: Harvard University Press.

Waldron, P. W., Collie, T. R., and Davies, C. M. W. 1999. *Telling stories about school.* Columbus, OH: Prentice Hall.

Welch, M. 1998. Collaboration: Staying on the bandwagon. *Journal of Teacher Education,* 49(1), 26–37.

Welch, M., and Sheridan, S. M. 1995. *Educational partnerships: Serving students at risk.* Ft. Worth, TX: Harcourt Brace.

Wiggins, G., and McTighe, J. 1998. *Understanding by design.* Alexandria, VA: Association for Supervision and Curriculum Development.

Wilson, M. 1993. The search for teacher leaders. *Educational Leadership,* 50(6), 24–27.

Wise, A., and Leibbrand, J. 1996. Profession-based accreditation a foundation for high quality teaching. *Phi Delta Kappan,* 78(3), 202–206.

Woolfolk, A. E. 1995. *Educational psychology,* 6th ed. Needham Heights, MA: Allyn & Bacon.

Wubbels, T., and Levy J. 1993. *Do you know what you look like? Interpersonal relationships in education.* Washington, D.C.: Falmer Press.

Index

There are
one-story intellects,
two-story intellects, and
three-story intellects with skylights.

All fact collectors, who have no aim beyond their facts, are

one-story minds.

Two-story minds
compare, reason, generalize,
using the labors of the fact collectors
as well as their own.

Three-story minds
idealize, imagine, predict—their best illumination
comes from above,

through the **skylight**.

—Oliver Wendell Holmes

SkyLight

PROFESSIONAL DEVELOPMENT

We Prepare Your Teachers Today
for the Classrooms of Tomorrow

Learn from Our Books and from Our Authors!

Ignite Learning in Your School or District.

SkyLight's team of classroom-experienced consultants can help you foster systemic change for increased student achievement.

Professional development is a process not an event. SkyLight's experienced practitioners drive the creation of our on-site professional development programs, graduate courses, research-based publications, interactive video courses, teacher-friendly training materials, and online resources—call SkyLight Professional Development today.

SkyLight specializes in three professional development areas.

Specialty
#

Best Practices

We **model** the best practices that result in improved student performance and guided applications.

Specialty
#

Making the Innovations Last

We help set up **support** systems that make innovations part of everyday practice in the long-term systemic improvement of your school or district.

Specialty
#

How to Assess the Results

We prepare your school leaders to encourage and **assess** teacher growth, **measure** student achievement, and **evaluate** program success.

Contact the SkyLight team and begin a process toward long-term results.

2626 S. Clearbrook Dr., Arlington Heights, IL 60005
800-348-4474 • 847-290-6600 • FAX 847-290-6609
info@skylightedu.com • www.skylightedu.com